Volume Three   Annual Edition

MERLYN'S PEN

Fiction, Essays, and Poems
by America's Teens

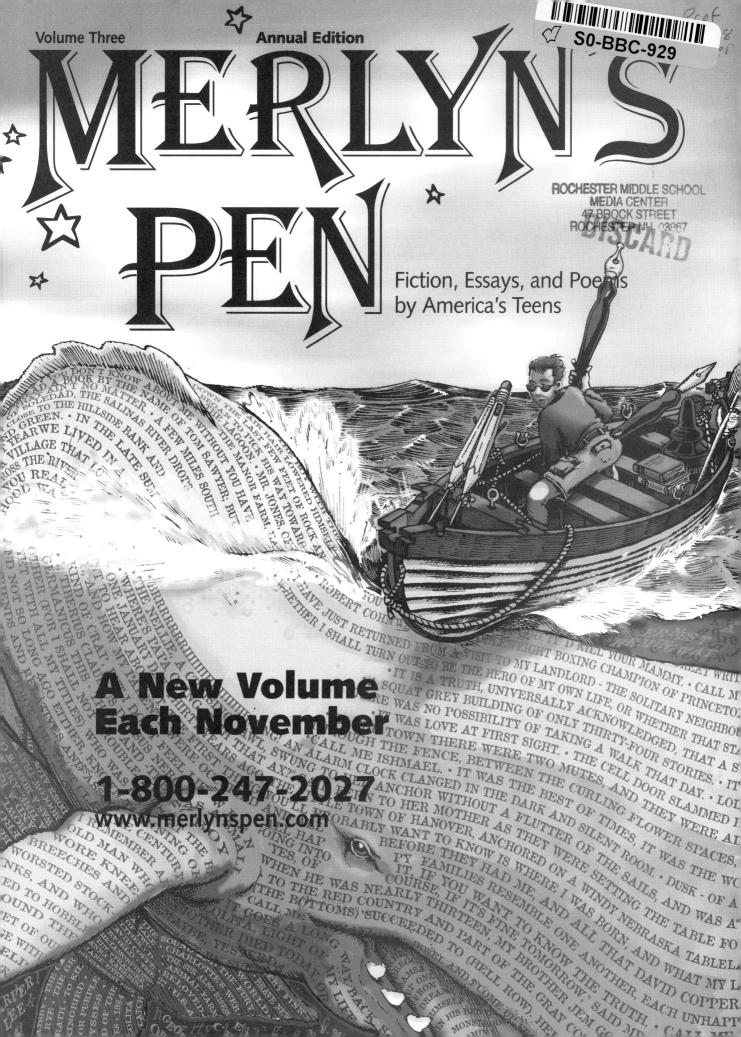

**A New Volume
Each November**

1-800-247-2027
www.merlynspen.com

CONTENTS

By publishing student writing, *Merlyn's Pen* seeks to broaden and reward the young author's interest in writing, strengthen the self-confidence of beginning writers, and promote among all students a positive attitude toward literature. The magazine seeks manuscripts that grip the readers' interest and stir the heart or mind. Highly valued are the authentic voice, manner, and clear expression of young adult authors.

◆ ◆ ◆

Information

The Pongee Stick

By Alex Taylor

contemporary
FICTION

We were having our big Veterans Day parade the day I got the call about Scott Henderson. Banners had been hung over the streets, and patriotism was a warm handshake floating in the breeze on every flagpole. Children ran from their mothers, husbands escaped from their wives, and autumn fled the approach of winter.

Somewhere on English Street, probably at Phil's Barber Shop, which was the only place in town where you could still buy RC Cola, a jukebox teetered on the edge of song. The WWII vets were there in force, sopping up the attention like some heap of rain-wrinkled rags. I could picture them all, their medals polished and shining, their uniforms dusted . . . They were proud men.

When I got the news about Scott, it was smudged and crumpled over the telephone voice of Tim Johnson. Tim was a heavy-eyed man whom I'd known for close to thirty years. Thirty years—God, it seems like such a long time. Long enough for a man to settle down and watch his grandson play Little League in the summer. Long enough for a man to lose more of his hair and his pride than he thought possible. Long enough to remember a few faces you knew when you were younger. And maybe, if you're lucky, a voice. Thirty years, and all we had was a box of photographs.

I was asked to pass the news about Scott to John Marshall, another of the names that linger in my memory, but I didn't. I had trouble passing it along to myself. Besides, John was old. His birth certificate wouldn't show it, but his face sure would. It would show the scars, the lines and highways of tears and worry. John was too old to handle the news about Scott, and I was thinking about how I was fully two years older than John myself. We were all too old.

There'd been four of us—Scott, John, Tim, and me. We'd left for the draft office on a clear white morning in spring '66, lured by the promise of Asian girls, hair black as ebony, and Vietnamese dope. The forests were said to be lush with it. There were stories of fortune, glory, and a free ticket to anyone who could carry a rifle and wade through the sea of rice paddies that was Vietnam. This was the paradise known as war, not the black-and-white evening news that showed U.S. troops dancing and singing because they were winning. At least, we were always *told* we were winning. We eighteen-year-old kids were being fed to the gooks like fodder in slow, methodical feasts. The truth is, we were going straight to hell.

We, what a simple, silly word. We, whose eyes and ears would be beating rich napalm and screams of death. We, fed fat upon lies and stories of how everyone but us would get jungle rot or have Charlie slice off their legs with his bayonet. We, who'd feel the cold swamps sucking into our wounds like leeches. We, kept awake at night simply to see the morning of our death. We, objects to be spat upon and forgotten, headstones in some faraway graveyard. We, who would get a quick handshake upon our return and, if we could afford it, a Nam bumper sticker.

After I got the call about Scott, I sat myself down in front of a rerun of "Gilligan's Island," letting the monotony of a laugh track settle with the Coors Light I was downing. I swallowed long, stiff gulps, like a kid taking his first drink. I was getting myself drunk and I didn't care. Didn't care because I had nothing left to do but *not* care.

On the magic screen, some bubble-headed blonde was endorsing some emerald green goo like it was a cure for cancer. Like it was going to save our souls from what happened in Vietnam, like it was going to take away our POW camps and asylums and flashbacks. Like it was the magic potion that would wash away all the bad, forgotten filth of war. I had a bottle of the stuff underneath my kitchen sink. The junk couldn't even cut grease all that well, but hey, at least it looked useful. All hail the great American detergent! I took another gulp and flung the can at the blonde. Missed. Got beer all over the floor.

I don't suppose anyone could have foreseen what would happen to Scott; if they did, maybe they thought it better not to say. Yet, looking back, I guess it was always there, a kind of sadness, even before the war. The future was there too, lying in wait of Scott Henderson, a tall plank of a man who carried himself in a perfect line, as if there was some invisible rope pulling him from above. Scott spoke

We'd left for the draft office on a clear, white morning in spring of '66, lured by the promise of Asian girls and Vietnamese dope.

only when spoken to, unless you were saying something about Nam, and then he didn't speak at all. It was as if his entire life was made of glass, and everything from schoolyard kisses to Nam itself just passed right through him. His hair was black and sooty like an old chimney flue. He used to run his fingers through that stuff all the time, us half-expecting him to pull out a sparrow's nest or God knows what else.

It was raining, as I remember, the day the thing happened, but then again, it rained every day in Nam. The rain

was usually nonstop, like a cold IV being dripped into us. But that day it was a whispering rain. The quiet of the jungle came with such a rain, a sloth-like lethargic quiet. Our troop, 85 Charlie Waters, was busying itself with the usual routine of playing cards, walking, toking, and then walking some more. We never seemed to get anywhere in that god-forsaken rice swamp; after four months of seeing nothing

It was a free ride into college and all the smokes we could ask for, right? God, what fools we'd been, our heads gleaming in the Vietnam sun like flashing neon road signs.

but the tops of our boots as we walked, heads down, we were all bored with Nam. But hey, it was a free ride into college and all the smokes we could ask for, right? God, what fools we had been, our heads gleaming in the Vietnam sun like flashing neon road signs.

Tim Johnson had set himself beside me that day. I can still see his eyebrows, hanging from his forehead like dead spiders—even more so when he was high. And Tim was always high. "Reckon they'll have us pansies walkin' this road for the rest of our born days, huh, Reg?" Tim always called me Reg when he was shooting the breeze in Nam, even though we'd grown up together and he knew my name was Kevin. But Nam changes things, even a man's name.

"Yeah, I guess they probably will, Tim," I chuckled. "But it sure is the easiest dang mile I ever walked." I don't think Tim heard a word any of us said, though; most times he just nodded and asked for another beer.

Up ahead, Lieutenant Waters was kneeling in the mud, the radio cupped in his hands like some precious gem. Looked like he was proposing marriage, I thought, muffling a laugh. "To all you raven-haired beauties out there, I, Lieutenant Daniel Waters, am asking for your hand in holy matrimony!" I imagined he was saying as his lips squirmed into the receiver. No one particularly liked Lieutenant Waters, his small, feeble mouth never breaking a line, his prim, gray hairs all tucked neatly under his helmet. He was a mechanical being, one who moved in a preprogrammed sequence the way a regiment of insects might. The army told him when to eat, when to sleep, when to take a leak and who on. To him, we were just a list of names and numbers, our lives his inventory. We would get them back, sure, but only after we did our share of killing and dying.

John Marshall, as I recall, was standing ahead of me a ways, looking down at his feet as if they were some grand and wondrous discovery. He took a few steps forward, his eyes not moving from those feet. "Walk, feet!" I could hear his pan-fried brain thinking, or at least attempting to think. This was all in a normal day's work for John, who was

Lieutenant Waters was a mechanical being, his every move preprogrammed. The army told him when to eat, when to sleep, when to take a leak. To him, we were all just names and numbers.

always stoned on grass or blatant stupidity, no one was really sure which. And then there was Scott, crouched by the roadside like some forgotten piece of furniture, set out for the trashman. He was listening to the stillness, to the rain falling on the foliage and the rice paddies. We were on the flattest, safest part of the road, but Scott seemed unusually edgy, his eyes moving in strange, jerky spasms. The road was dirt, of course, and on a high rise above the jungle, which made ambush nearly impossible. The road was nice. No hidden bumps or ditches. No sudden drop-offs or landslides—just pure mud-caked road. The road was nice, I was thinking, because it made you feel nice, made you feel secure. It was a good road.

There was no doubt, though, that today we were on a part of the road which was unknown to us. After about a half-hour of idle walking and rain-watching, we came to a bend in the road where it veered off at an odd, roller coaster angle, inhibiting sight. This was not like the other roads we'd been on. I wondered what was up, then realized how silly that would sound if I said it out loud, and laughed a little nervous chuckle at myself. Lieutenant Waters stopped us and stood looking at the bend for a long time, as if he hadn't expected it to be there. I could tell he was rolling the sight of it over and over in his mind, inspecting it like a new car. The bend made him uneasy; we all could see that by his constant fingering of the radio receiver which hung limply in his hand.

He swallowed his fear, though, like you always do in Nam, and replaced it with a dumbfounded frown, a frown that meant he had either pissed his pants and was ready to die, or that he just didn't care. Then he waved us on, but

only for a few steps, because there, dead ahead, was a small tunnel cut into the ground. It was a nozzle of a hole, barely big enough for a man to fit through, but Lord knew Lieutenant Waters was going to make us try.

I looked at Scott. We both knew what that tunnel meant. It meant ammunition stores, booby traps, and maybe even an infestation of gooks staring into the darkness with little gook eyes, ready to cut us in half. Scott and I knew that danger, the silent, wet horror of the tunnel. We were tunnel rats, half-witted idiots who scrambled into dark, briny tunnels, our only hope being to come out at the other end with all our arms and legs. Sometimes, that was all that was left of a tunnel rat—just pieces. It was quite an interesting sight to see, I suppose, us arming ourselves with only a flashlight and 9 mm, then slithering into the tunnel and disappearing inside as if it were our refuge.

The tunnels were usually abandoned; it was the booby traps you had to watch out for. For all the primitive weaponry and techniques that those gooks used, they sure knew how to mangle and cripple a man. Pongee sticks were what tunnel rats feared. They were so simple you had to almost laugh the first time you saw one. Just this crudely dug pit in the middle of a tunnel, barely ten feet deep, with all these bamboo spikes sticking up at you like pointing fingers. It looked pretty silly, actually, like something out of a Tarzan movie, until you smelled what was on those sticks. If it wasn't the remains of a GI, it was always that sickening buffalo dung they smeared on the sticks; when you smelled that, you realized just how ingenious the whole thing really was. Those gooks not only wanted to kill Americans, they wanted to infect us with gangrene and make us lose a leg or arm.

John Marshall was looking down at his feet as if they were some grand and wondrous discovery. "Walk, feet!" I could hear his pan-fried brain thinking.

A man might only get a pongee through his leg or arm, but then there was that smell, just like a rice field rotting in the sun, and he knew he wasn't coming home in one piece. I saw a man get skewered by one of those God-awful pongee sticks. It got him right through his left thigh, blood spurting up from the pit like a geyser. There was nothing but fear in his eyes when we pulled the stick out—no pain or hate, just pure, icy fear. He knew he'd never walk again or play catch with his son on a sunny afternoon. But I don't think that's what really got to him; it was that rotting, sewage smell of the buffalo dung eating his leg away.

"Henderson, McDonnell! Get your butts up here, you pansies, and rat this tunnel!" Lieutenant Waters was his usual cordial self. I looked up ahead and could see his little cherry head, hard-boiled and well-done, angrily staring at us as if we were gooks ourselves. Both me and Scott began to move to the front of the platoon, our comrades gawking and parting for us to pass. I'm not sure if they were admiring our stupidity or our bravery, but we always gave 'em a good show. It was child's play, really, play that sort of lifted the dull haze and dope smoke of Vietnam. Every time me and Scott ratted a tunnel, I could always see the fear in everyone's eyes; though many times, I could have sworn that what I saw was envy.

The tunnel called to us in its blatant openness, like some gaudy spring flower. Lieutenant Waters stood eyeing us, his tight fatigue collar seeming to choke him. He looked very old to me at that moment, very old and stately, like he was already drawing his army retirement pension.

It was my turn to tunnel first that day. Scott had gone ahead in the last one, which had turned out to be a muddy snake hole featuring two dead rats and a few mortar shells. It was customary that tunnel rats have a certain bond, if for no other reason than that the other could plan ahead for his partner's mistakes. But it was different between Scott and me. Ours was a silent communication of mutual feedback

that happened partly because Scott never spoke and partly because talk spooked and distracted us. Although we never really knew each other, you could feel us *wanting* to know each other. Wanting to shake hands at our kids' ball games and talk football and why the bass weren't biting this year.

We were tunnel rats, idiots who scrambled into dark, briny tunnels, our only hope being to come out at the other end with our arms and legs still on us.

Wanting to get on with the business of becoming ourselves, yet still remain a little bit of each other.

The tunnel smelled ruthless as it flapped over me like fetid old mold. Rich, black VietCong mud slid over my fatigues as I groped onward into the darkness, my flashlight a mere flicker of hope. I could hear the nervous, cattle-like shuffling of the platoon outside. Scott was coming down behind me, squirming rigidly in the tunnel. There was

Archaeology, Circa 1892: Jews on the Lower East Side of Manhattan

Here the revolutionaries had their last dinner.
Careful archaeologist, you can see the traces
of their loud conversation and warm potato food.
You can see the Lower East Side
   that they tracked in on the mat
   as they stomped in from the winter.
The cold scalp smell of their caps,
   their loud chapped hands.

You can see their footsteps,
but the kitchen is still invisible
where the women cooked with silent dark eyes
and short sturdy necks dipped slightly down
in the careful sustenance of every day.

Their shared strengths lie in the twist of their necks,
hard and used to damage—
the women from looking down and in,
and the men from looking forward.

—*Nava Etshalom,*
Eleventh grade, Masterman School,
Philadelphia, Pennsylvania

[*Other works by Nava Etshalom appear on pages 58 and 85.*]

nothing down there that I could see—just walls, alive with the gaunt possibility of jungle rot. The prospect of seeing one's feet slowly digested inside out by jungle rot is why

Those sticks looked pretty silly, like something out of a Tarzan movie, until you smelled what was on them: it could be the remains of a GI, or that sickening buffalo dung.

most GIs kept their feet drier than whiskey breath. This was a crude hole, the kind dug by frantic, pawing Vietnamese, but there was a kind of planned expansiveness in its crudeness. Long billows of bleakness seemed to beckon, as on some New Orleans bar strip.

Yes, we were scared, but on this kind of day, when the rain was suspended in sad little mists and the sun was in hiding, we welcomed the tunnel. It was our only escape. Every tunnel had that same smell of dirt and decay, a scent that made you feel almost primitive. It alone could lull you into a state of total escape. Looking back at the tunnel entrance, we could see the damp Vietnam sky receding behind us.

Once Scott was all the way down we proceeded, conveyor-like, through the canopy of tunnel. We had to kneel a whole lot, as the roof of the tunnel almost always grazed our heads, forcing us downward. Fear sucked at us like a vacuum from both ends of the tunnel, but we had never turned back and we weren't going to start today. I suppose we were more afraid of turning our backs on our fear than the fear itself. There was no sound within the tunnel as we drew ourselves deeper and deeper within, almost embracing it. Our hands ran delicately over the thick sod walls, looking for tripwires or secret rooms where ammo might be stored.

There was a slight pause before it happened, that event that molds each of my waking and dreaming moments. I like to think of that pause as me paying a sort of unseen toll for my future, whether it be for sunny beaches and lazy, tall cocktails or the hard, machine-smelling labor of a factory. We all pay a toll to get to tomorrow; we just don't recognize it until we look back over our shoulder.

There was a snap of dirt and branches as the ground beneath me fell through, almost sluggishly, the day I paid my toll. I'll never forget that sound. It couldn't have been more than a second before those pongee sticks were pointing at me, but it seemed eternal. At night, as I lie listening to the slow rhythm of my wife's breath, or when I'm walking down the street with my grandson in tow, I can still hear that slow, unearthly snapping of ground giving way, can still

see that whirlwind of dirt and swirling bamboo leaves.

I can remember thinking, in that split second, that in the eternity of that moment I could even see them, staring up at me like the guns of a firing squad. How long had they been waiting? Weeks, months, years? But they had had all the time in the world, waiting, wanting, and then I had come along, bopping around the Vietnam bush like a fraternity boy. And they, those pongee sticks, were going to taste of me.

I thought I heard Scott muffle a little cry, sucking in his breath, but then again maybe he had screamed, or said nothing at all. I

Dear Brother

Did you know the last time I saw you,
You were already gone?
Your black shirt withered into a
Black horizon.
You said,
"It's here. I have to leave"
But thought,
It's time to go.

There was the room we shared,
Remember,
Fireflies by the windows, blinking bright while
We watched the face of evening.
Blue to violet, now
The very darkness dreaming.
There, under tender bedcovers,
Peace flowed from the stories we told,
The truth under the stars.
We drifted in its waters,
Bathed in its waves, two princes
Awaiting the coming of day.

I watched you leave.
And sometimes now, without you, I feel
I am being squeezed out of something.
I become afraid because it will finish,
And I will be in the middle of dryness.
Will I be like you,
Or like a purple conch that lies broken
In my own hands?

—*Aalap Mahadevia,*
Twelfth grade, Phillips Exeter Academy,
Exeter, New Hampshire

guess it doesn't really matter if he screamed or not; what matters is that no one else but Scott was there to cry, scream, or say anything at all. Fiery pain exploded at my every nerve, and I just knew that my legs were being devoured by the pongees and their dung venom. I had wanted them to get only my legs, but I had forgotten the terrors of gangrene and living life with only one shoe and having to put on my pants sitting down. I couldn't see anything, not the tunnel, or Scott, or the pongees. All I could see were two stubs jumping and twitching where my legs should have been. It was the fear, I know, since I can walk and squat all I want now, but for a split second, what I had were stubs. I thought of my wife back home, her perfect face looking down at my two bloody stubs. I saw my mother, old and smelling of chamomile, wobbling off through her flower garden without me by her side to support her.

But now there was dirt pouring into my eyes and this must have startled me back into consciousness. I looked up from the pongee pit and saw my hands, gripping like hinges to the muddy edge. Scott was holding on to my fatigues and looking completely calm and collected, as if he'd done this all before. "Don't move," he said firmly, his eyes glazed. Beads of sweat trickled from his brow as he tried, with all his fear, all his hate, and all his love, to pull me out of that hole. "Don't move," he had said, but when I think of it now, maybe he was telling himself not to move, not to run away. He was afraid; I could see it when his lip quivered, but he would never leave me. Scott would sit there, inches above those pongees, holding onto me until they found a cure for gangrene, if need be. That's just the kind of man he was.

I must have drifted in and out of dreams because all I remember after looking into Scott's stricken eyes was being dropped to the ground, just as his exhaustion got the better of him. I don't know exactly how long he held me up out of that pit—could have been fifteen seconds or fifteen years—but, Lord knows, to this day I still can't see how he held my 250-pound body suspended above those pongees. And I'll probably never understand how it was that the pongees never even touched me. Scott had caught me, even before I had fallen. He knew the pongees were there; he could smell them. All I can remember after it was over is just sitting there in that cold, embryonic tunnel, staring in disbelief at my legs, whole and untouched. And Scott beside me, his silence smiling as if to say, "Bet you'll never figure this one out." And I never did.

There's really not a lot to say about what happened after Nam, except that we all got a little older and a little wiser, but I guess you've heard that one before. John stayed home, here in Georgia County, and ran a successful newspaper until all the stories dried up. I don't know if there were really any stories that John found, just people who cared. Maybe people stopped caring. Tim went to college to become a lawyer, but he never made it. We'd lost touch over the years and that phone call was the first I'd heard from him in a good ten years. And me? Well, I just stayed here working weekdays at the Swifty Stop 'n' Go. Some men never settle into their homes; I never really settled into a job other than pumping gas for old ladies who drive big Lincolns, and changing oil for guys in business suits. But it's Scott I want you to know about.

The tunnel smelled ruthless as it flapped over me like fetid old mold. Rich, black Vietcong mud slid over my fatigues as I groped onward into the darkness.

We never told anyone what happened in the tunnel that day, even though it's against platoon policy, and I don't suppose we ever will. A man has only so many secrets in his life, a few of them that he'll take to his grave. But I just can't let it die altogether, and that's why I'm putting it down here, on paper, for someone else to hear. Besides, somehow I think that Scott would have wanted it this way. After the war, he just seemed to get cold and passive, not really wanting to die, but wanting to live in a world he had left behind.

This symbol next to a poem means that you are reading a classic from the Merlyn's Pen collection. If you have a favorite Merlyn's Pen poem to recommend for reprinting in a future issue, send an e-mail with the title of the poem and the name of its author to merlynspen@aol.com, or call the editors at 1-800-247-2027.

Merlyn's Pen classics appear in this issue on pages 26, 43, 45, and 66.

Maybe *he* was the one trapped in that tunnel all those years ago, and maybe he never got out. Anyway, all I know is that we all got old and that we were seeing less and less of Scott as the years went by. After the war he just seemed to drift away like a sea fog, never to return.

I woke up in a cold sweat the night before Scott shot himself. I'd had a dream, maybe a nightmare even, but couldn't remember it. I just knew that I had to call Scott, and was halfway through dialing his number when I stopped myself. I didn't even know the man that I was calling—never really had. I don't know if even Scott himself did. So I hung up and lay in the stillness, thinking. I thought about all the dreams we'd shared, all the promises we'd made to ourselves and to each other. And you know, I couldn't remember a single reason for any of those dreams or promises.

I guess I should have finished dialing that number. Maybe it would have stopped him, but maybe it wouldn't have. Or maybe he was still in that tunnel, waiting for me to come make some magical appearance and remove him from the pongee sticks of memory. Scott had gone on to save a dozen more lives in Nam, then returned for a second tour—God only knows why. I guess he knew Vietnam was his only life. Even though it was killing his closest friends, it was keeping him alive. He had to stay. Maybe he knew there'd be no one to pull him out of that one long tunnel we've all got to face, even though he had been there for so many. But for all the medals and uniforms Scott wore, he was naked after Nam. We've all got to face the pongee pit sooner or later; it's just that some of us don't have anyone to pull us back out. ★

Creation

A segue!
Yes!
That's it, that's what we need. A segue.
OK, so a segue into . . . the story . . . into . . .
the beginning . . .
A girl . . .
A girl with kaleidoscope eyes!
Yes, that's brilliant. Vivid. Familiar.
Beatles song.
Are we allowed to do that?
Of course! It'll be like a joke.
A joke! Is this a comedy?
A comedy. A drama. A mystery. A . . .
A patchwork! A patchwork orange.
A clockwork orange.
No, that doesn't work at all.
So, back to the kaleidoscope eyes . . .
Yes. What would that mean anyway?

Well, what does it conjure? What do you see?
Psychedelic muffins.
Come on!
I see . . . I see . . .
A girl. A young girl. Impossible to decipher, easy to
persuade.
Indecipherable!
Indecipherable but impressionable!
More, we need more. What do you see her doing?
Emerging. Emerging from . . .
From inner depths, from inside, from . . .
Behind a tree!
That works.
What does she look like?
Beautiful. Young. Naked.
Oh, God, come on.
No, I really see her naked. No kidding.
OK, naked. I can deal with that. Naked with pride or
with shame?
She is beautiful, but wait . . . I see her running.
Escaping!
Escaping. A girl with kaleidoscope eyes escaping . . .
No! Escaping with a girl with kaleidoscope eyes!
So who else is escaping?
A man!
Nude?
Wouldn't she be uncomfortable if he wasn't?
OK, we've got two nudes.
They've gotta do something . . .
Cover themselves, maybe?
Cover themselves with . . .
Fig leaves.
Fig leaves I can see!
That's what I meant, at first, anyway.
OK, so nude except for the fig leaves. They're both
escaping.
Why would anyone want to escape with only fig
leaves for cover?
If there was some unspeakable outrage, they might be
forced to.
Force, force . . . force is good. I like force.
So they were thrown, to take force a step further, out
of perfection.
Into . . .
A desert.
A desert of loneliness in a field of shame!
Loneliness! Shame!
They run from perfection to a desert of loneliness . . .
In a field of shame. Yes, this is it!
So what do they do? Where can they go from here?
They'll have to tell us that.

—Elizabeth Green,
Ninth grade, Montgomery Blair High School,
Silver Spring, Maryland

The Merlyn's Pen 1999 Short Story Contest Winners

First Place—Senior Division
(Grades 10-12)
LORAINE REITMAN—"Virginia Mud"
$500 prize

Loraine Reitman wrote "Virginia Mud" as a junior at Annandale High School in Annandale, Virginia. The story grew out of a writing workshop exercise called a 'word pool' in which students chose random words from books, magazines, and song lyrics. "Most of us creative writing students chose words like 'serendipity' and 'ephemeral' and 'cacophony,'" she says. "I chose 'milk,' 'cotton,' 'suck,' 'mud,' 'drip,' and 'spigot.'"

Loraine took up writing in sixth grade out of boredom and restlessness, but she really got serious about writing in eighth and ninth grade, following the death of her aunt. She cites Percival Everett, Octavia Butler, Mercedes Lackey, Sylvia Plath, and Wally Lamb as favorite authors.

Loraine plans to major in creative writing in college and hopes to pursue writing as her primary source of income. "To prepare," she says, "I am learning to cook from scratch and knit my own sweaters."

First Place—Middle Division
(Grades 6-9)
DAN KAHN—"The Felicity Maker"
$500 prize

Dan Kahn, of Plainfield, Vermont, is 15 years old and a student at U-32 Junior/Senior High School in Montpelier. He wrote and submitted his story in the ninth grade.

Dan says "The Felicity Maker" is one of his first real attempts at writing short fiction. He was inspired to try his hand at writing when he read about the Merlyn's Pen short story contest on the Merlyn's Pen web site. As a new writer, Dan found his contest win both surprising and encouraging. "Being published by Merlyn's Pen," he says, "is a terrific and unanticipated honor."

Dan is active in community theater. He likes acting, singing, playing piano, and reading fantasy; favorite authors include H.G. Wells, J.R.R. Tolkien, and Ray Bradbury.

Second Place—Senior Division
(Grades 10-12)
JOSEPH REYNOLDS—"Lucky"
$250 prize

Joseph Reynolds wrote "Lucky" while in the tenth grade at the William Penn Charter School in Philadelphia, Pennsylvania. For a complete profile of Joseph, turn to page 34.

Second Place—Middle Division
(Grades 6-9)
SAM HANCOCK—"The Gift of Life"
$250 prize

Sam Hancock wrote "The Gift of Life" while in the ninth grade at the Canterbury School in Fort Wayne, Indiana. For a complete profile of Sam, turn to page 33.

Read the Stories ➤

Virginia Mud

By Loraine Reitman

contemporary FICTION

Afternoons in southern Virginia were spent at an unnamed pond where Chase and I would go when it was hot. It was the only pond I knew of that wasn't crowded with steaming cows or flocks of geese soiling the water—probably because it was so fully hidden by bushes and trees. Chase and I spent nearly every afternoon there before cold set in (which is more time than my neighbors in Maine can imagine). So my return to Virginia found me slipping through the brambles to find my childhood.

The soil made a gentle transition to mud, then sloped beneath thick reeds to turn into black gravy. It was so hidden under delicate thorn bushes that I was splashing my sandals through water before I realized where my feet had led me. Bending down, I pulled my sandals from the watery mud, and then from my dark dripping feet. Mud sucked between my toes as I held my dress up from the water's edge. Virginia mud is like heaven under your feet.

I made my way around the edge of the pond and came to a gap in the bushes where I could walk ashore without running into more needles. The pond was twenty yards across, five deep in the middle. I pulled the combs out of my hair and placed them on a velvet moss stone next to my sandals. My dress was a toe-touching, cotton-flowered, button-down favorite, now splattered with mud. I slipped it off and laid it carefully across the bushes. My bra followed the dress; then came nylons, noticeably torn by my walk, and then my watch.

"Hurry up, Chase!" I called.

I turned and waded into the clear water, which churned up in dark clouds wherever I stood. Chase was still off in the bushes, pulling off that silly bow tie and dress shirt his father made him wear to Sunday school. The mud was billowing up through the water as I sank lower into the pond and made a few tentative strokes. I curled my feet close to my body to avoid the cold water at the bottom.

As always, the most wonderful moment of my swim was sinking my steaming head and hair beneath the surface. I listened to Chase fumbling around in the bushes as I closed my eyes and tilted back under the warm water.

My hair flared out around me as I pushed myself lower, closer to the cold water hidden beneath the surface. My scalp and skin tingled as water coursed through my hair and over my face. My feet found gooey black mud, and I opened my eyes to the hazy underwater world, then pushed my way back to the surface. A glint of gold had caught my eye.

Even as my head broke the surface, I was pulling in air to go back down. The gleam was probably trash, I guessed, as I dove again to the bottom of the pond, this time headfirst. It could be trash. Or treasure.

The water was dark with mud now, the black mud

Chase was somewhere in the bushes, pulling off that silly bow tie and dress shirt his father made him wear to Sunday school. "Hurry up, Chase!"

from the bottom. Insects and bits of reed and grass were churned up as well, making it harder to see the golden shine. I dove down till my fingers could reach out and twist into the bottom reeds, anchoring my whole body to the floor.

Even in the murky water I could make out the thin stretch of light. I pulled myself through the reeds and icy water until my face was just inches from the treasure. The golden light was a tiny circle of metal, no bigger than a coin. I pinched it even as my lungs began to ache from holding in so long. The ring was caught in the heavy grasses, but I pulled it close enough to see the design—plain, with the initials C.L.

My feet pushed off from the bottom and launched me to the bright warm world of oxygen. Brown water dripped from my chin and nose while the water from my hair blinded me. I knew who the ring belonged to. Sucking in air, I shouted for Chase.

"Your ring, Chase! You dropped it in the pond!" Behind me, I could hear him plunging into the water by the shore.

I dove down again, finding my spot at once in the dark waters. I hadn't fully caught my breath yet, but I held my lungs tight and reached for the glint. My hand closed around the cold metal, and I began yanking. Hard. I could hear Chase in the water above me, splashing as he came toward the center of the pond. I looked up to see him, but the water above me was empty. The sun was shining through the water like so many golden pebbles. I breathed out slightly, watching the bubbles float quickly away. I had the oddest desire to breathe in.

Sliding my hands along the reeds, I slipped the ring onto my left ring finger without looking at it. I was ten. Convinced that Chase's ring belonged there, on that finger. Not on Shirley Gregory of Ohio, twelve years

later. My eyes stayed shut, my body enjoying the cool beneath the water. Somewhere above me, Chase was floating on the surface. But he was supposed to be at the bottom of the pond, with me.

My lungs didn't ache anymore. I slid back and realized that the constant draw of the surface pulling at my body had disappeared, that I could relax into the comforting black mud. The golden pebbles dripped down on me from the dark above. As the rest of the air slid out of my lungs, I leaned back, my hair twining with the grasses. My movement sent up a thick cloud of darkness to surround me. I could feel the suction of the sticky mud along my back and thighs.

Chase was swimming closer now; I could feel the water churning around me as he dove deeper. And then he was touching me, pulling my arm up to the surface. He didn't understand how comfortable it was to lie on the black bottom beneath the grasses. I opened my mouth to tell him and felt cold pond water rush into my lungs. My eyes opened, saw Chase's frantic face. He was kicking wildly, not understanding why I still clung to the reeds. He turned and stared at me, his soul in his eyes.

I turned and slipped off the ring, freeing myself from the strong grip of grasses. The golden loop dropped back into the black mist, back into the dark reeds. And Chase pulled me steadily back to the sunlight and oxygen.

I came to the surface with lungs thick and watery, convulsing. My throat choked for air, my chest burned for oxygen. I kicked wildly in the center of the pond to hold myself above the water. And when my vision cleared and I could breathe well enough to pull myself to one side, I couldn't help noticing that Chase was already gone.

As the rest of the air slid out of my mouth, I leaned back, my hair twining with the grasses.

I walked out of the pond, covered in mud and debris. I had forgotten about certain nasty realities. Like bugs. And slime. And how itchy mud gets when it dries. I was still dripping as I pulled on my watch and bra, left the nylons that a fat black spider was now inhabiting, and stepped into the dress. I buttoned it up, refastened my hair, snapped on my sandals and turned back to make my way to my brother's house. Perhaps I'd give my condolences one last time to Shirley. But I was ready to go home. ★

Search here for works that relate to your grade level and to popular topics and genres. Indexed works sometimes are written by students in grades above or below the suggested reading audience. For example, a 10th-grade student might write a story for readers down to grade 7. To select stories only by the author's grade, see the author profiles beginning on page 32. In the Index by Topic and Genre, poems are *italicized*.

Index by Interest Level

Index by Topic & Genre

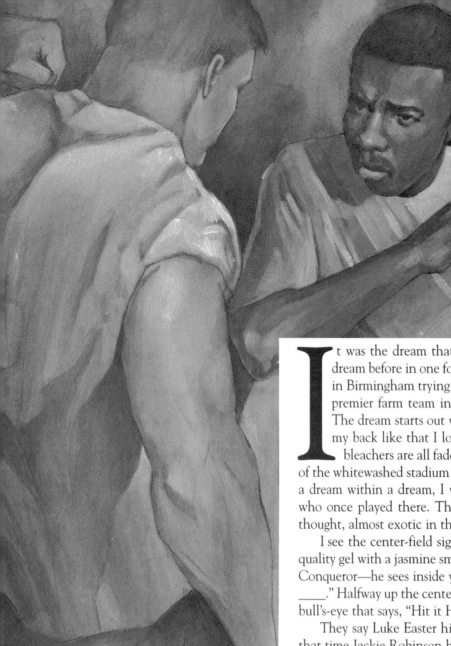

Lucky

By Joseph Reynolds

contemporary FICTION

It was the dream that got me excited and woke me up. I've had the dream before in one form or another. This time I'm seventeen and back in Birmingham trying to make the baseball team. The Bombers are the premier farm team in the Negro League and competition is difficult. The dream starts out with me on the grass doing inverted bicycles. On my back like that I look around at the beat-up old stadium. The pine bleachers are all faded and dusty. The yellowed woodgrain framework of the whitewashed stadium shows through the paint and the dirt and, as if in a dream within a dream, I watch the frolicking black ghosts of the legends who once played there. Their motions are efficient and independent from thought, almost exotic in their beauty.

I see the center-field signs in my dream, too. "Tucker's Hair Pomade—a quality gel with a jasmine smell"; "Get your daily number from High John the Conqueror—he sees inside your soul"; "Bentley's Dance Hall—from 10 until _____." Halfway up the center-field flagpole, there is a four-by-four-foot-square bull's-eye that says, "Hit it Here. Win $250."

They say Luke Easter hit it the year he went up to the white league. By that time Jackie Robinson had been with Brooklyn for two years. The white league had been reaching down every now and then and drafting hot colored prospects. By 1949 every major-league team except the Phillies had a colored boy on its farm team or its major-league squad. I wanted more than anything to elevate my game and get noticed before the white league dried up for colored prospects.

This particular morning, my dream featured me doing sprints. I pulled a groin muscle and fell in slow motion onto the cinders. The trainer floated casually over to me.

"You hurt, Lucky?" he drawled.

They call me Lucky. William's my name. William Luck.

"Naw, boss," I groaned. "I'm OK."

I looked at my crotch. My inner thigh, where I had pulled the muscle, swelled up until it was the size of a basketball. Then it exploded with a gushing liquid roar. Blood sprayed everywhere, even on the "Hit it Here" sign two hundred feet away. That's how I missed the majors in my dream that morning. It was always the same—a physical injury—but always a different injury. My dreams never had me failing from mediocrity, and this morning was no different.

When I jolted awake, my inner thigh was cramping from the long day's drill and I had sweated through the sheet. My eyes focused on the springs of the sagging bunk above me, traveling from one square to another, tracing geometric figures before I allowed my mind to accept two disturbing realities: that I

accepted two disturbing realities: I'd never become a major-league baseball player, and I'd soon be going to war.

would never become a major-league baseball player, and that I would soon be going to war. My eyes welled up and salt stung my sun-scorched cheeks. In the musky darkness I relived my failure to make it in the big leagues.

The Bombers eventually cut me and sent me back home to Selma. When I went to get my old clothes-pressing job back, a girl from Georgia had taken the job—"until I get on my feet," she sniffed, as if clothes pressing wasn't good enough for her. I went to the Navy recruiter the next day. They promised me a job in a battleship kitchen as a cook's helper. I couldn't see myself helping a Navy cook, so I considered my options and showed up at the Army recruiting office that same afternoon.

When my platoon first came to Fort Benning, Georgia, in the early summer of 1950, we were all green and hostile. Most of the men were drafted and each had a story to tell that involved the injustice of his call to arms. Just me and Callahan were enlistees. Job Callahan was a huge, nut-brown boy of eighteen with a shy, pleasant smile. He and a big white boy named Hinshaw were from Arkansas and they were as different as a cat is from a dog. Hinshaw was brash and imposing and did not compromise. Callahan was unassuming, but had an air of self-confidence about him. Both were appointed squad leaders along with George Jelinek and a tough street kid from Brooklyn named Rizzo. They were all chosen because of their obvious size and strength. Jelinek, called "Jelly Neck" by the drill instructors, was mysterious. He didn't talk about himself. In fact, he didn't talk at all. He seemed stupid but he did everything easily.

The first few weeks of camp were little more than a continuation of the first few horrible days. We ran everywhere that we didn't march. The fort was hot in August and afforded no privacy. We showered and shaved together and there was much striving for a pecking order. After a few weeks we began to accept our plight and resigned ourselves to the numbness of discomfort as a way of life.

Then, for a reason that I didn't understand until years later, the pressure eased. The drills were no less draining, the tedious cleanups of the already immaculate barracks were still demeaning, and the interminable berating and harassment by the drill instructors was just as humiliating. But the resilience of youth is the essence of adaptation: we saw equal suffering in our comrades and adjusted.

So there was a settling. We began to form into groups based on race, parts of the country, and common interests. We developed a wary tolerance for one another and in rare cases struck up friendships independent of our little groups. The squad leaders separated themselves from the main body of the troops. They enforced the will of the DIs and sought few outside friendships. Each squad leader controlled twenty or so men in the eighty-man platoon, and for the most part they were passive. Callahan and Rizzo were lax in reporting any but the most egregious violations of regulations. Jelinek wanted no part in any activity that involved controversy. His strength remained implied and he ended challenges to his authority with a long stare and a few slow shakes of his huge head. Hinshaw took immediately to the role, and as time passed he began to relish it.

Jelinek was mysterious. He didn't talk about himself. In fact, he didn't talk at all. He seemed stupid but did everything easily.

One day I was polishing my belt. The ammonia cleaner made me lightheaded and caused my eyes to tear. I ran outside for air, forgetting my open footlocker. In the Army an open footlocker attracts thieves, so there is a minor penalty for the infraction called an Article 15. The squad leaders were instructed to take an open footlocker to the DI's office for "safekeeping." Hinshaw took mine.

When I came back inside, still teary-eyed and gasping, there was a hush in the barracks. I missed my locker immediately and asked for it. There was a short silence; then a boy called Rabbit stuttered, "H-H-Hinshaw t-t-took it to the office."

The DI's office was at the opposite end of the two-storied barracks. One group of forty men occupied the lower floor and forty the second.

"DI s-s-says the onliest person w-w-who can get the locker is the person who brought it in," stammered Rabbit.

I turned to Hinshaw. "Get my locker, will you, man?"

We ran everywhere that we didn't march. Fort Benning was hot in August and afforded no privacy. We showered and shaved together . . . and began to accept our plight.

"Can't," said Hinshaw. "DI says you got to come to the office." Hinshaw lolled in his bunk, a hulk of a man in the fullness of his youth. His face was flat and ruddy; the corners of his thin-lipped mouth turned down. He was sullen and calculating. His slitlike eyes regarded me from under his cap brim.

I turned and took the long walk up the aisle past the frightened faces of the men, each of them knowing that any of them could be in my place. They sat on their lockers busily pretending to groom their areas. I knocked once hard on the office door. A harsh, deep, Southern voice sounded like a shot.

"Get in HERE!"

I entered two steps and stood at attention. Three white men, all in their late twenties, sat around a small table playing cards. The closest to me was silent while I was in the ten-foot-square room. The man who sat nearest the single window was angular and straw blond. His eyes were blue and cruel.

"Whaddayou want, *boy*?" The military requirement that one at attention must have his eyes straight ahead was a relief to me.

"I want my footlocker, sir."

"You ain't got no goddamn footlocker in here, boy!" he thundered. I knew voices. This one was from the Deep South, the hill country. The loathing for me was in his voice and his excited breathing.

"Yes, sir, I do," I said. "It's right there." I pointed to it from attention, my eyes riveted to the wall. I

could feel the fear in my stomach and lower bowel.

The third man spoke. He was the head DI, Corporal Brescia.

"What's your name, boy?"

"Private Luck, sir." My fear betrayed me and my voice cracked. I tightened my buttocks and my abdomen.

"Well, Private Luck," he started in a singsong Southern drawl, "Private Hinshaw brought that locker in here for us to watch." His eyes lit up and he regarded his associates with a smirk.

Corporal Brescia was short and muscled almost to deformity. His uniforms fit snugly and every muscle demonstrated itself independently. He was swarthy and obviously Italian. Italians were rare in the Deep South. He was only the third or fourth I'd met.

"But it's my locker, sir." I tried persuasion, sensing that I was going through some script that they had already written.

"*Hinshaw's* locker!" exploded Corporal Brescia as he jumped to his feet. He came to within an inch of where my face would have been but for his lack of height, and screamed into my chest. "It's Hinshaw's locker and he's the onliest son of a bitch that's gonna take it outta here! You understand that, you pigheaded piece of whaleshit?" Flecks of spittle sprayed my face and for an instant my eyes dropped to his raging jaws, then shot back to the wall above his head.

I did understand. The script was unfolding.

"May I be excused, sir, to get Private Hinshaw to liberate my locker?"

Three white men, all in their late twenties, sat around a small table playing cards. One man was angular and straw blond, his eyes blue and cruel. "Whaddayou want, *boy*?"

Corporal Brescia stepped back a pace and grinned up at me. "Now how in the name of Jumpin' Jack Shit are you gonna do *that*, boy?" he mocked, his face ominous and glistening through a thin film of sweat. The anticipation in his bearing was clear. His voice was husky and his breathing rapid.

"I'll do it, sir," I said without any idea as to *how* I

would do it. "May I be excused, sir?"

"Get your dumb aborigine ass outta here," he said in disgust, then pushed me backward out of the office and slammed the door. I could hear them laughing contentedly behind the door.

I slowly walked the eighty feet down the aisle to where the squad leaders sat by my bunk. They had heard every word and sat expressionless as if each had been asked a difficult question. They watched me expectantly as I moved toward them.

If anyone understood at all, it seemed Callahan did. He looked up at me sympathetically. I fought the temptation to ask him what to do. Rizzo regarded me from beneath lowered lashes. His lips were trembling. He looked down when I caught his eye. Jelinek was the only one standing, his arms folded across his chest. I got to the point.

"Hinshaw, get my locker."

He stood up to six-feet-five inches and grinned wryly.

"Sheeeit!"

"Hinshaw," I said, "you get my locker out of the DI's office or I'm gonna kick your ass." I hoped my voice did not betray my doubts. I knew I could fight. I considered myself on the fringe of being a pro athlete. I had fought for every privilege or inch of turf that I'd gotten in my young life, but slim at six feet tall, I had real concerns about whether I or anyone

1985

Open casket
gray swinger suit
skinny maroon tie.

Thin lips. spread like butter
against ivory face—
thicker. than real life
creamier than real skin.
Dead.
No longer watching,
resting,
makeup changing.
Reality blurring a child's last memory.

It was such. a long time ago.

—*Jessica Koenig,*
Twelfth grade, Iola-Scandinavia High School,
Iola, Wisconsin

could dominate Hinshaw physically.

"Sheeeit," he scoffed again.

"Let's go down to the latrine," I invited.

Hinshaw scratched his square jaw and leered from behind his hand at a small cadre of sycophants who raised their eyebrows and snickered. They feared him absolutely. The latrine was in the basement under the first-floor quarters and was the spotless shave and

I cowered in muddy foxholes. I slept in the snow. I watched a stateside-bound cargo plane shudder under the weight of Callahan's aluminum coffin.

shower room for eighty men. I turned and walked toward it. Every man in the platoon came with us. When I entered the huge bathroom with its thirty sinks lined in a row and ten toilets on the opposite wall, I waited at the door. Hinshaw strode in with a smirk of curious confidence. I closed the door behind us and heard the muffled scramble for viewing space at the transom above the door.

I moved to the center of the floor. Hinshaw, as if preparing to learn a dance, moved with me.

"Go get my locker, man," I said a final time. He looked at me dully, his arms bowed out to his sides, as if preparing to grapple.

"I ain't gettin' sheeit," he said as if surprised that I would repeat the demand.

My first blow was a stiff left jab that hit his forehead. His eyes crossed for an instant. He appeared disoriented and reached out his arms as if to get a hold on me. I backed up and, at arm's length, hit him with a second left to the forehead, crossing with a right to his jaw. His knees buckled as he lurched forward and supported his weight on a sink.

I realized at that moment that Hinshaw could not fight at all. He had probably never fought before. He was only in the latrine because I had challenged him, and he had only taken my footlocker into the DI's office because he wanted their approval. Still, I had to get my footlocker or suffer a summary court-martial for dereliction.

"Hinshaw," I tried again, "get my footlocker."

"I ain't gettin' squat, boy!" He touched his lip and looked curiously at the bright blood on his fingers.

I had no wish to hurt him, but I hated him for hating me. We were both puppets, dancing for the DIs. I prodded my normally gentle nature and started my right fist toward his jaw. He turned and dropped his head, taking the blow on the nose. Blood gushed from it onto both of us, and Hinshaw fell into a sitting position, dazed and bewildered.

I walked on unsteady legs to the DI's office, but when I raised my hand to strike the door I saw the darkness of my fist and hesitated. Fear made my stomach convulse, and gastric fluid scalded my

"You ain't got no footlocker in here, boy!" he thundered. I knew voices. This one was from the Deep South. The loathing for me was in his voice and his excited breathing.

throat. Trembling, partly in rage at my trepidation and from fear itself, I knocked at the door.

"Who!?"

"Private Luck, sir."

"Goddamnit, boy! I tol' you Hinshaw got to get that footlocker!"

"He can't, sir." I could smell my sweat.

"Why the hell can't he . . ." The door opened and Corporal Brescia recoiled at the blood on my shirt. "Jesus," he gasped as if in prayer.

At that moment Hinshaw wobbled by us on the landing, a blood-soaked towel pressed to his face.

"Jesus," Brescia breathed again. He pulled me into the room and closed the door. All three looked at me through alternately wide and narrowed eyes. Quietly, Brescia said, "Get your footlocker outta here." He set his beefy hands on his hips. "You're the platoon leader now. You report directly to me. Understand?"

"Yessir," I answered, realizing that somehow I had blundered my way to the end of the script.

I walked the aisle to my bunk, past four dozen sets of awestruck eyes, to pack and move my equipment into the large room next to the DI's office. The irony of the situation caused me unspeakable ambivalence. Thereafter, the DIs and the other men treated me with quiet respect akin to reverence. Other young soldiers on the post who did not know me would turn to face me when I passed their little groups, and step aside and speak my name—"Hey, Lucky." His very size and appearance of brutal power had once given Hinshaw the same favored treatment. Stories of our confrontation passed from platoon to platoon and

were embellished and exaggerated. One version had Hinshaw hospitalized after a two-hour struggle.

The truth, of course, was known only to a few, the whole truth only to me—and I said nothing. Inwardly, though, my personal humiliation made me reflect on the nature of humanity so intensely that I developed a philosophy which, if not profound, was certainly mature. I began to look at all people as either decent, shallow, or striving. Those who were decent deserved my friendship and respect. Those who were striving toward decency, a decency which included gentleness and honesty, were on hold. Those who were shallow were encouraged to strive.

Strange that it comes as an afterthought, but I did go to Korea. I stood in the open hatch of a troop plane and I jumped when the loadmaster slammed his icy hand on my shoulder and screamed, "GO!" I cowered in muddy foxholes. I slept in the snow. I watched a stateside-bound cargo plane shudder on takeoff under the weight of Callahan's aluminum coffin.

And then one day it was over. The Chinese poured back over the Korean hills they so coveted, and we were packed up, all but a police force, flown to the Philippines, then home. My baseball dream was replaced by a dozen others, which I soften with yellow and green pills and therapy at one Veterans Administration hospital or another . . . It isn't really over.

Someday, when my head heals up, I'm going back home. Right about now, though, I feel like I've been beaten with barbed wire and left for dead. But I'm a survivor. There's something in me that just won't let me give up no matter how bad things get. I'm going to go home and get my baseball gear out of Momma's cellar. I'll be twenty-one next month and I'm going to take me another shot at the League. They don't call me Lucky for nothing. ★

MERLYN'S PEN
The National Magazine of Student Writing   Grades 6-12

Cover Sheet for Submissions

Everyone in grades 6-12 may contribute.

Important

Send up to 2 works per author at a time, <u>each work attached to its own Cover Sheet</u>. Manuscripts must be typed, double-spaced, no page limit. You may combine "Response Only" and "Response & Critique" submissions in the same mailing. Submissions are considered for both *Merlyn's Pen* and the American Teen Writer Book Series. Please do not send art. As of Sept. 1, 1999, manuscripts submitted without a current Cover Sheet (this one or later) cannot be returned.

A2000

Step 1: Check the Merlyn response you wish to receive:

☐ **Response only.**

Please enclose a $1 postage/handling fee for each manuscript.
You'll receive a response from Merlyn within 8 weeks. This cover sheet and an acceptance or rejection letter will be returned to you, but your manuscript will not. (Make a copy!) Please do not send a stamped, self-addressed envelope; Merlyn's fee includes one.

☐ **Response & Comprehensive Critique.**

For each manuscript you wish an editor to critique and return to you, please enclose $5
($1 post./handling plus $4 editorial critique fee). This service, which takes 10 weeks, brings you a comprehensive editorial response (over 100 words). Your manuscript will be returned to you, with comments, with your acceptance or rejection letter.

Please do not staple money. Please do not send coins.

Step 2: Authors must provide all of the following information in ink:

◀ In this box, type or print **Author's Name** and **Complete Home Address** (name, street, city, state, zip).

Title of Work: _____

Merlyn's Pen cannot respond if your submission is missing information or is illegible.

Step 3: Fill in the blanks in ink:

AUTHOR'S GRADE _____ AUTHOR'S AREA CODE AND PHONE _____

SCHOOL NAME _____

SCHOOL ADDRESS _____

CITY _____ STATE _____ ZIP _____

SCHOOL AREA CODE AND PHONE _____

ENGLISH TEACHER _____ PRINCIPAL _____

Classroom Teachers: Feel free to send the work of several students in one large envelope. Attach a cover sheet to <u>each</u> piece and indicate the requested response. Enclose the appropriate fee.

Published students receive three copies of *Merlyn's Pen* plus payment. **Poems** above 50 edited lines $50; below 50 edited lines $20. **Fiction/Nonfiction** up to 1500 edited words $20; over 1500 words $50; over 3500 words $100; over 5000 words $200.

Send manuscripts, each attached to its <u>own</u> cover sheet, plus fee (no coins, please) in one envelope to:

Merlyn's Pen Submissions, P.O. Box 910, East Greenwich, RI 02818-0910   Tel: (401) 885-5175

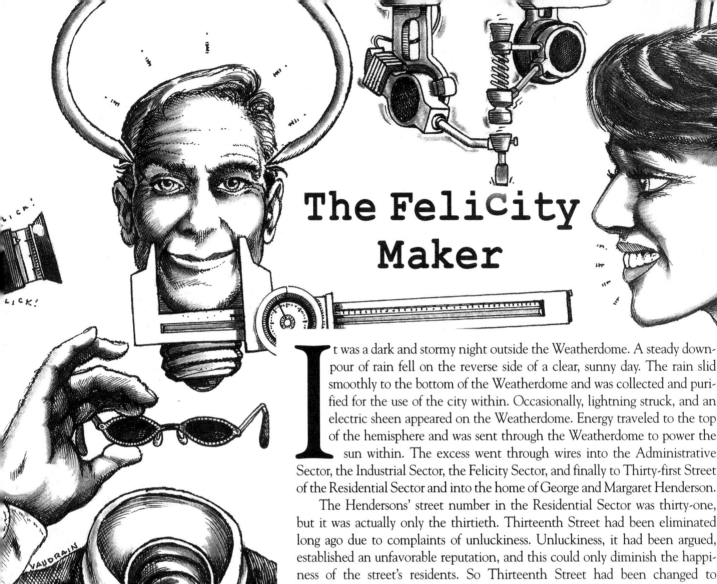

The FeliCity Maker

By Dan Kahn

SCIENCE
FICTION

It was a dark and stormy night outside the Weatherdome. A steady downpour of rain fell on the reverse side of a clear, sunny day. The rain slid smoothly to the bottom of the Weatherdome and was collected and purified for the use of the city within. Occasionally, lightning struck, and an electric sheen appeared on the Weatherdome. Energy traveled to the top of the hemisphere and was sent through the Weatherdome to power the sun within. The excess went through wires into the Administrative Sector, the Industrial Sector, the Felicity Sector, and finally to Thirty-first Street of the Residential Sector and into the home of George and Margaret Henderson.

The Hendersons' street number in the Residential Sector was thirty-one, but it was actually only the thirtieth. Thirteenth Street had been eliminated long ago due to complaints of unluckiness. Unluckiness, it had been argued, established an unfavorable reputation, and this could only diminish the happiness of the street's residents. So Thirteenth Street had been changed to Fourteenth Street, Fourteenth to Fifteenth, and Thirtieth to Thirty-first. But all this had occurred before anyone could remember. And in any case, street names were not what was on George Henderson's mind.

George was in the comfort of his Comfort Chair, thinking about birthdays. It was, after all, the twins' birthday today. They would be home from their Felicity Sector schooling in fewer than ten minutes.

George stopped thinking. It would be an awful shame to get up from his Comfort Chair; it was one of the many pleasures of life inside the Weatherdome. Its ultra-padded covering provided automatic rocking, massaging, and optimal coil resistance. Besides, the birthday preparations would be handled through computed administrative procedure. The twins would receive a random gift to stimulate felicity, as they had for the past twelve years, twelve months, and twelve days. There was no telling how old they really were, for George and Margaret both were the same age as the twins. The very thought of old age had a way of depressing residents of the Weatherdome, and to stop counting after the number twelve seemed as good a time as any.

It was at that moment in George Henderson's dormant thought process that Margaret and the twins entered through separate doors. George glanced at his watch, which was always the right tightness and never left red imprints of the wristband on his wrist. It was twelve fifty-nine: time to cycle back to one.

"Happy birthday, Jennifer!" exclaimed George in the extremely felicitous tone with which he always spoke. "Happy birthday, Thomas! Happy birthday,

Margaret!"

They all echoed his tone to each other and to him. It was, after all, everyone's birthday today. Just like yesterday.

Without further ado, they proceeded from the spacious living room where most of their interactions occurred to the special gift room with festive gift wrapping for wallpaper. With felicitous anticipation, they reached into their respective present boxes. George had received a set of several attractive and unique stamps to complement his collection. No one knew what purpose a stamp held, but the collecting of stamps was deemed by all to be a safe and felicitous hobby. Margaret's hand met with a bouquet of dew-covered white roses. Jennifer sighed. She had received only a deluxe box of imported chocolates. Again. Had she not been a tiny bit disappointed and had she searched the box, she would have found no origin of importation anywhere on it. Thomas's eyes grew wide as he beheld a long green-and-yellow tube. The Hendersons had no term to describe and no appropriate felicitous feeling to accompany this strange tube with the words "Super Soaker" displayed prominently in a large, explosive font.

Thomas had barely taken hold of the thing when a hole appeared in the center of the gift-wrapped ceiling. A tractor beam emerged and shuttled the troublesome object to the confiscation room, where a large incinerator pit lay waiting. After a few minutes, the incident was replaced in their minds for the time being by more felicitous thoughts.

It was nine-fourteen in the evening. The thunderstorm on the outside had finally ceased one minute ago, at nine-twelve. The sun was directly overhead, as it had always been, and no clouds could be seen in the bright blue sky. And speaking of weather, Margaret Henderson was, at that moment, at the library in the Felicity Sector. She was looking for a book on the weather.

"Where might I find the meteorology section?" she inquired of a library clerk who looked particularly good-tempered on this fine sunny evening.

"Modern or ancient?" asked the clerk, smiling.

"I don't know. How about ancient? Which would you advise?"

"I'll write down both number codes for you," replied the clerk resolutely.

"I beg your pardon? Both number codes?" asked Margaret, befuddled at the slip of paper she had just been handed.

"Yes, both books. Modern and ancient meteorology."

Margaret broke off the chat and set about looking up the books. The chat had been bordering on making her appear stupid, and that would have been most infelicitous.

Of course, there were only two books in the ten-story library on meteorology. What a narrow, boring topic it was! But whatever her motives, she was now committed.

Margaret took the elevator to the third floor, where the modern meteorology book was located. She found the number in no time. Opening the very slight volume, she beheld three incomplete sentences on the only page.

Sunny. Clear skies. Seventy to seventy-three degrees.

Now Margaret Henderson was truly puzzled. Why had she chosen meteorology, of all topics? And what had possessed her to look up modern meteorology? Any child knew that it was always sunny with clear skies, and with highs and lows from seventy-three to seventy degrees Fahrenheit. Shrugging off these troublesome thoughts that were bound to lead to infelicity, she again boarded the elevator and instructed it to go to the ninth floor.

The ancient meteorology book was as large as the modern one was small. She decided to check it out, pressing the button labeled "C" that was found on the back of all library books. Instantly, an identical book appeared next to the original. She picked it up and walked home.

The walk was not necessary, but it was very pleasant in the sunny, seventy-degree weather. She was thinking of children at that moment. The novelty of twins was finally wearing off and she was considering the appeal of triplets. Not three new children, obviously, but two more Jennifers. She had agreed with George long ago that their future children should be mainly girls. Triplets would make life so much more interesting. This time, she would take the easy-install option. Custom install could be so bothersome, after all. Why should she and George waste time customizing their new children—as they had with the first two—when easy install could pack in all the memories and experiences

The very thought of old age had a way of depressing residents. To stop counting after the number twelve seemed as good a time as any.

instantly? She would definitely bring this up with George later that night, or the next day—whenever they decided to retire.

George and the twins were in the yard when Margaret returned home. They had spread a red-and-white checkered tablecloth on the ground and waited for Margaret before opening the mysterious picnic basket which had been randomly selected from a host of meals. The twins now tore into the basket with ravenous hunger. It contained four quite ordinary slices of mega-chocolate cheese-cake, which had been refined and fortified years earlier to contain all essential nutrients but retain its unhealthy taste. Margaret joined them, and they ate their cheesecake in silence.

The Hendersons had no felicitous feelings to accompany this strange tube with the words "Super Soaker" displayed in a large, explosive font.

Silence, as always, bred dormancy, which bred drowsiness, and soon they had all fallen asleep where they sat.

The visual scanning mechanism of the surveillance cameras noticed the opportunity, and the brain-wave probing mechanism confirmed it. It was not often that such an opportunity arose, where all witnesses to a relic of the Infelicitous Ages had fallen asleep simultaneously on the same lawn. Such opportunities were usually generated, as they so rarely occurred naturally.

The opportunity was sent through the wiring immediately. It passed down Thirty-first Street and the Residential Sector, went straight through the Felicity and Industrial Sectors, and proceeded cautiously into the Administrative Sector. Even such abstract things as opportunities had to be cautious inside the Administrative Sector. Felicity was its goal, but not its means of achievement. The opportunity came to rest with hundreds like it inside a computer that was not the only one of its kind. This wealth of opportunity was housed in a nondescript, windowless skyscraper and overseen by Martin.

After seventeen years, Martin could say in all honesty (although it would stimulate no felicity in others to boast so) that he was good at what he did. He had just returned from correcting the faulty memories of a meddlesome youngster who had been sure she had seen graffiti in a back alley of the Industrial Sector. Even with the sector's reputation for lagging behind the times, such evidence of the Infelicitous Ages was unheard of. Martin found it intriguing that however many steps were taken to ensure the grip of felicity on the masses, something always slipped through. Anyhow, the little girl now realized how very wrong she had been. She had not seen any evidence of violence or vandalism or vulgarity. No, Martin corrected himself. She had not realized anything. She would go about her felicitous existence as though nothing had ever happened. What a thankless job, working for the Department of Opportunity!

The next case involved some faulty technology in the Department of Birthdays. He would speak to his superiors about that. The encryption employed by the Department of Birthdays and sent to the Industrial Sector had been created after the Infelicitous Ages. Still, one recipient had received a greeting concerning old age and drooping body parts. Yes, it really was odd how these things kept slipping through.

Martin would finish this next case and have lunch. It would be an early lunch, before midnight, but this case would be a quick one. Not nearly as difficult as the graffiti. With all luck, those poor slumbering fools would not have the slightest idea about the original purpose of the "long green tube."

Thomas popped one eye open. It was a beautiful sunny morning, or was it still night? He glanced at his watch. No, it was morning—quite late, in fact. They had slept past four. But time didn't concern Thomas Henderson, for he was feeling more felicitous than he had in months. He leapt up and roused the others.

The picnic basket had been mysteriously refilled during the night and now contained chocolate éclairs. Thomas ate his breakfast hurriedly, as he professed desire to be off to school. Jennifer declined to make the journey with him, but Felicity Sector schooling had no time constraints; students came and went as they pleased.

Thomas proceeded in andante fashion down the street. He was unencumbered, as usual. Whatever materials he required for learning would be provided in the

Shakespeare

Shakespeare, did you live in the sea?
The beauty of the salty, unsmooth waves is yours
    beating roaring rhythms on the shore
    where tides have come and gone.

I am caught by your waters
that shape their path through stone.
    The wind drives them into a hundred
    tumbling, hurtling curls of thought.

Shakespeare, were you ever haunted by a storm?
Or did you laugh with calm lapping,
    flowing with a foamy lightness,
    leaving a crescent imprint on my sand?

—Joanna Hearne,
*Tenth grade, Lincoln Park High School,
Chicago, Illinois*

Felicity Sector.

The Felicity Sector boundary was clearly marked: it was where the colors became freer. It was not uncommon to see a scrambled rainbow of buildings on any given block in the Felicity Sector. Another sign of the change was the presence of more andante students, wearing felicitous smiles.

One particular student caught Thomas's eye on this particular morning. The girl was several years his junior, and looked away when she sensed Thomas's gaze. For some reason, she reminded him of something that, for one reason or another, lingered at the back of his mind and refused to come out.

Intrigued, he made his way through the throng of students that was thickening as it approached the school, but by the time he got to her location, she had wandered off. He banished the thought from his mind.

The schoolhouse, being the only one of its kind inside the Weatherdome, was a far shot from the one-room schoolhouses common to the Infelicitous Ages. It was a good thirty stories high, with floors separated by topic.

Entering a small elevator (there were several dozen), he turned to find the girl making her way toward him. He held the elevator long enough for her to board, then quickly pressed the "close door" button.

"What floor?" he asked her simply. As he said the words, his eyes locked with hers, and he noticed that, while gleaming brightly in a felicitous manner, her eyes seemed to portray a felicity that was only superficial. He had never heard of an unhappy person before, so he quickly discarded that laughable prospect as a trick of the dim elevator lighting.

"Writing," she replied.

"What a coincidence," he said, lying. He had been

What had possessed her to look up modern meteorology? Any child knew that it was always sunny and seventy to seventy-three degrees Fahrenheit.

planning on spending the day in the clever-diversions section of the felicity-break floor, but he punched the writing button anyway. The elevator surveillance cameras detected his lie amongst other transactions, and sent the information along to the Administrative Sector for storage.

The writing floor was the same as it had always been, with its Comfort Chairs behind a ring of student desks.

The teacher was a hologram in the center of the ring that faced all angles. It would show any images required, and used a built-in voice that had been designed to be both soothing and engaging.

Thomas and the girl took adjacent Comfort Chairs and waited for the ring to fill up with students. As the roll

Triplets would make life so much more interesting. This time, she would take the easy-install option.

neared completion, the hologram in the center began to whir.

"Writing is a most rewarding pastime when carried out in a selectively felicitous manner," said the voice. The hologram flashed images of smiling children writing felicitous literature.

"Today we will be studying a technique called 'reminiscence'. Instead of recording present or future felicity, I want you all to record some felicitous events that occurred yesterday." Words appeared on the hologram as the computer went about its writing. No one was excused from the assignment, as doing so would diminish fairness and felicity.

What felicitous events had happened to Thomas on the previous day? He had been cleverly diverted for many school hours, eaten several deliciously unhealthy-tasting meals, and fallen into a blissfully dreamless sleep on the sunny lawn. All were pleasant thoughts, and Thomas began setting them on paper. None tarried in their instantaneous flow to the monitor in front of him, save one: his birthday gift.

After fifteen seconds, everyone had finished. Writing was a carefully honed skill that involved none of the frilly philosophical and depressing psychological analyses that covered thousands of pages in the Infelicitous Ages.

It was then time to critique. The hologram displayed each student's entry individually, and students were allowed five seconds in which to offer their input. The hologram always gave the form response, "Your writing is an inspirational work of felicity worthy of your pride." The five seconds was merely formality, as the eloquence of the computer summed up all aspects of the work.

Thomas experienced his second bout with the concept of infelicity when the girl's writing was displayed on the hologram. It was a blank page. The hologram delivered its form response and quickly shifted to the next entry, a piece on an especially felicitous birthday, but the girl appeared visibly shaken and entirely infelicitous at her failure of recollection. The last time Thomas saw her was the next day, when she wore a broad smile and was obviously oblivious to the previous day's discontent.

Martin found it intriguing that however many steps were taken to ensure the grip of felicity on the masses, something always slipped through.

It was unfair. How could Jennifer Henderson be expected to share her living space with two new siblings? One would have been one too many… but two? It was all the fault of her materially insecure mother and her indecisive, incompetent father.

Her grumbling was bordering on infelicity, so she ate a pint of ice cream and closed the inner debate. There was no use disturbing herself; her parents made their own decisions without her input. Besides, the siblings were already on their way. In fact, they had just arrived.

They were late—three seconds past the five-minute guaranteed delivery. She would make sure her parents claimed rightful compensation for the injustice.

"Mother! Father! We're home!" chorused the new twins in a naively felicitous way.

Jennifer decided on felicitous courtesy and entered the living room, where Thomas and her parents had been waiting for five minutes and three seconds. She took a seat in a Comfort Chair and tried to establish an air of superiority.

The new twins entered, equipped with their own airs of superiority that had been easy-installed several minutes earlier. They had reason to be every bit as snooty as their clone, who had spent twelve years, twelve months, and twelve days being custom-installed; the new twins had accomplished all that and possibly more in just five minutes and three seconds.

"Jennifer! Jennifer!" exclaimed Margaret. Six eyes turned toward her, but she chose not to notice. "How felicitous to see you! I dare say you were worth every bit of the extra three-second wait!"

The easy-installed twins both gave their parents a hug and sat down in the two new Comfort Chairs that had been delivered after Margaret placed the order for the twins. They took their seats in the same tired, relieved fashion as the custom-installed twins, a triumph of modern programming which helped ease the transition anxiety of the parents.

"I have planned a relaxing evening at the Felicity Sector Circus for tonight," burst out Margaret, eager to finalize and smooth over the filial transition. "I hope you four can put aside your petty installment differences."

All professed desire to attend and a lack of interest in perpetuating lines of installment distinction, but the custom-installed Jennifer secretly could think of no more pleasing fate than the removal of these impostors.

Martin did not like to be kept waiting, but this special circumstance required his patience. He had been waiting over three hours for the Felicity Maker, a clear indication of the balance of power between the two. Martin felt especially privileged because (in his own mind) he was not being summoned; he had requested the meeting personally because he felt that his carefully worked-out conclusion transcended normal protocol in which he would forward all information to the next level of power in the Department of Opportunity. After all his extensive following of opportunities, he had come to the conclusion that all these infelicities slipping through were the result of a massive computer encryption error which would require urgent addressing.

"Enter!" said a booming voice.

Writing was a carefully honed skill that involved none of the frill philosophical and depressing psychological analyses of the Infelicitous Ages.

Martin wasted no time in jumping out of his non-Comfort chair and scurrying through the great gold doors, where he immediately prostrated himself at the foot of a solid-gold table.

At the head of the table sat an ageless man. Through daily rejuvenation sessions he had managed the longest benevolent reign in all history—some two hundred-odd years. Rejuvenation, although a top priority during the Felicity Maker's natural life span, was withheld from the general public for fear of overpopulation. The general public's engineered ignorance of mathematics—aside from the basic reading of street numbers and clocks—would ensure felicity in the case of overpopulation, but (luckily) the Felicity Maker had been educated in the Infelicitous Ages. He alone had foreseen the trouble math might cause in the future. The formula for the continuance of a benevolent reign required that all a person's views be changeable for a felicitous outcome. As long as the public had no knowledge that one times one makes one, the Felicity Maker could make the product two or zero without diminishing greater felicity.

"Martin, I have been hearing great things about you," began the Felicity Maker in a tone Martin decided harbored distinct ominousness. "I have watched your career for a very long time, ever since you were easy-installed thirty-nine—I'm sorry, twelve years, twelve months, and twelve days ago. You have become very proficient at your work in the Department of Opportunity. Tell me … do you enjoy your work?"

"Yes, Felicity Maker," intoned Martin, without raising his head. "Serving the greater felicity in general and the Department of Opportunity in particular gives me great pleasure."

The Felicity Maker nodded. "And would you continue to do so?"

Congratulations

I guess I should say
Congratulations.
You're the only guy who's ever made me feel
Like a week-old filly
I saw in a paddock
With oversized, knobby knees
And tiny pointed hooves
A short neck
And donkey ears
Who couldn't get her feet in line.
So all her spindly legs went
Every which way
Except forward.
She wobbled along
Trying to coordinate that ungainly body,
To find a rhythm in her steps,
And I wondered if she was embarrassed
That the other foals could run and jump
While she was still learning to dance.

—Jennifer Bedell,
Twelfth grade, Blue Valley High School,
Stilwell, Kansas

"Oh, yes!" said Martin without reservation. "Nothing would be more felicitous!"

"I shall respect your wishes then."

Martin ventured a glance at the omnipotent figure at the head of the table. Could it be that he had detected a hint of tiredness in that ageless and indefatigable voice? For one instant he became the first in many years to meet eyes with the peculiar man at the head of the table who, inside

"The secret that must never travel beyond this room is that absolute felicity is an impossibility."

the Weatherdome, was the very essence of omnipotence. And what he perceived in those horrible, deep black eyes shocked him.

"Yes, Martin," began the Felicity Maker in a soft, chilled voice, shifting his gaze to the golden table. "I know why you are here. Your half-baked theory is not entirely correct."

There was a long, awkward pause. Martin could hear the Felicity Maker sighing and softly moaning, as if deliberating a great risk. This went on for several unbearable minutes, and then his pains were rewarded by more talk.

"I am going to do something to you that I have never done to anyone before, Martin: I am going to confide a great secret in you. Your theory is partly correct. There is a glitch of sorts, enabling all sorts of minor infelicities to fall through. But the cause of this glitch is no encryption error and exists despite two centuries of attempted eradication. The secret that must never travel beyond this room is that absolute felicity is an impossibility."

The Felicity Maker looked at Martin to see what seismic impact this statement was having on him. Martin was guarding his thoughts very well, but his mental fortresses were no match for the technological ingenuity of the surveillance cameras. The Felicity Maker knew he had confirmed one of Martin's darkest fears.

"Oh, certainly," he went on in a more casual tone, "certainly we may work toward the goal of absolute felicity—as we have done for many years. We have managed to achieve perhaps 99.9 percent felicity, thanks to the constant vigilance of the Department of Opportunity and constant innovations in the social departments and Felicity Sector. In another hundred years, perhaps we will have 99.999 percent felicity, but we will never achieve 100 percent, however close we may come. Forgive me for using mathematical terms, but am I not correct in my knowledge of your illegal self-instruction on the subject? Ah, I thought so. I do not hold it against you. Perhaps, in this final hour, you may reach a better understanding than I. I only understand the concept vaguely: Nature is somehow creating infelicity. It will not allow us to reach the absolute felicity value. The closer we come, the more we are working against nature."

Martin was now visibly shaken by this confirmation. He was experiencing true infelicity at that moment. All he wanted was to escape this hopeless, meaningless life. His wish was deferred to the Department of Opportunity.

"What a marvelous circus!" exclaimed the easy-installed Jennifers.

The circus was a giant, ten-ring affair. It contained everything from a clown juggling fifty random objects (an elephant was not uncommon) to "Fluffy the Flying Ferret." Needless to say, the entire show was produced by holography.

"I've seen better," remarked the custom-installed Jennifer in a confrontational tone, which was recorded by the surveillance cameras.

"Well, so have I!" said an easy-installed Jennifer defensively, the desired effect sought by the other Jennifer. "Though I have only just entered this family, my past experiences are no less significant than yours."

A Perfect Specimen

I caught a dragonfly today.
Its wings were veined in silver,
eyes iridescent,
each leg properly attached.
A perfect specimen.

It struggled with frantic energy,
scrabbling for freedom
to flit and gyrate over limpid lakes,
to dance with Terpsichore.

I cupped my hands around it,
clutched its fragility.
Still it flung its frail body
against my palms,
unwilling to surrender,
unafraid of a foe
who could crush it in a fist.

I deposited this delicate hero
into a jar to slowly suffocate.

—*Dorrie Karlin,*
Eleventh grade, Hopkinton High School,
Hopkinton, Massachusetts

"But you have no experiences."
"Have you?"

Fluffy the Flying Ferret made an especially low dip that neared the Hendersons, and both children ceased their chatter. In the closest ring, a dazzling array of acrobatics was taking place, acrobats performing dizzying leaps and stunts unaided by trapezes and safety nets.

The custom-installed Jennifer refused to talk with the impostors bearing her name, which was of no concern to them.

It was of concern to George Henderson, who was befuddled at all this seeming infelicity. He had never heard of it. Certainly children in his day would never dream of behaving in such a fashion! What of morals? What of respect and integrity?

Margaret was looking again at the acrobatics ring. The fringe around the ring was a series of spikes that resembled the ancient meteorological symbol for a "cold front" (she had been digging around in her meteorology book of late). How sad that the only weather she would ever know was sunny, clear skies, seventy to seventy-three degrees.

As Margaret Henderson brooded in her roomy circus Comfort Chair in the Felicity Sector, massive amounts of electricity were being consumed by the holography. This was of no consequence: there was an especially violent thunderstorm releasing shard upon shard of high-voltage lightning on the reverse side of a clear sunny day. An electric sheen was omnipresent on the surface of the Weatherdome. Energy traveled to the top of the hemisphere, and was sent through the Weatherdome to power the sun within. The excess went through wires into a hospital in the Administrative Sector, where in room 507 Martin was sleeping soundly, dreaming of opportunities and his approaching birthday. There was still a good deal of leftover energy, so it proceeded out of the hospital, through the Industrial and Felicity Sectors, and finally to Thirty-first Street of the Residential Sector and into the home of George and Margaret Henderson. When he awoke in the morning, George had only one thought: It was the quadruplets' birthday today! Margaret thought of dew-covered flowers and how pleasant a diversion the previous day's circus had been. The custom-installed twins thought of deliciously unhealthy-tasting meals and felicitous schooling, and the easy-installed twins did much the same, to the greater felicity of all. And the house of the Hendersons was felicitous once more, and that was good. ★

SHORT STORY CONTEST

The editors of Merlyn's Pen magazine (since 1985) and the American Teen Writer Series of books (1996) each year read submissions from up to 12,000 teen writers in grades 6-12. Fewer than 75 of these works earn publication in Merlyn's Pen, which is enjoyed and studied in English classes and libraries internationally. Students whose works appear in Merlyn's Pen receive $20 to $200. Merlyn responds with an encouraging letter to every contributor, published or not. Students seeking publication must use the Merlyn's Pen Cover Sheet, printed in every Merlyn's Pen magazine and in Merlyn's catalogue and website: **www.merlynspen.com.**

Merlyn's Pen reads submissions for publication all year long.

Top Prize $500: One **first prize of $500** will be awarded in each division: Middle (grades 6-9) and Senior (grades 10-12). Up to two **second prizes of $250** may be awarded in each division. Prize-winning stories will appear in Merlyn's Pen, published every November, and in the **teen area at the Barnes & Noble website, bn.com.** All contest entries will be considered for publication in Merlyn's Pen.

Contest Description: Story length must be between 600 and 7,500 words. All topics and story genres, including personal narratives and "true" stories, are welcome. Multiple entries by the same author are welcome; each entry must be stapled to its own Merlyn's Pen Cover Sheet. Follow the instructions on Merlyn's Cover Sheet; choose either the "Response Only" or "Comprehensive Critique" option.

Deadline: Entries must be postmarked by **March 1.** Merlyn's Pen will respond by May 25. This contest will run twice, in 2000 and 2001. The March 1 deadline will apply in both years.

Eligibility: Students must be in grades 6-12 or the equivalent in home or international schools.

How to Enter: Staple a **Merlyn's Pen Cover Sheet** (see Merlyn's Pen magazine, catalogue, bn.com or www.merlynspen.com) to each entry. Follow the directions on the Cover Sheet: select the "Response Only" or the "Response and Comprehensive Critique" option. Do not send a stamped, self-addressed envelope: the $1 fee includes one. There is no additional fee to enter the contest.

Mail your entry to the address on the Merlyn's Pen Cover Sheet and add this line to the address: **"Story Contest Entries."** The Merlyn's Pen Cover Sheet is printed in Merlyn's Pen magazine, in Merlyn's catalogue (page 15) and website: www.merlynspen.com. For more information, please e-mail merlynspen@aol.com, or call 401-885-5175.

For all other correspondence:
Merlyn's Pen: Fiction, Essays, and Poems by America's Teens, 4 King Street, P.O. Box 910, East Greenwich, RI 02818
E-mail: merlynspen@aol.com

Daniel Becker lives in Chesterfield, Missouri, and created "Sweaty Palms" while a **junior** at **Lafayette High School** in **Bellwin, Missouri**. He enjoys listening to punk/ska/hardcore and attending concerts; on weekends he plays paintball and ushers at his neighborhood movie theater. Daniel's favorite authors include "the usual suspects, like Vonnegut and Shakespeare, but also Raymond E. Feist, Timothy Zahn, Robert Jordan, and Isaac Asimov."

Mia Cabana wrote "There But for the Grace" during her **sophomore** year at **Ludlow High School** in her hometown of **Ludlow, Massachusetts**. Like her protagonist, Mia has been playing clarinet since grade school; she's also an accomplished saxophonist. Active in student government, she has served on Student Council and as vice president of her class. Mia sees a future of acting and/or costume and set design.

Jim Cady wrote "Fire and Water" during his **junior** year at **Arlington High School** in his hometown of **Arlington, Texas**. The son of missionaries, Jim spent his early years among the Masai in the bush country of western Kenya, where he was homeschooled in English and Swahili. Grades seven through ten were spent at boarding school, also in Kenya. Returning to the United States for his final two years of high school, Jim is happy to be back, and enjoying the many creature comforts and electronic outlets. Active on the Web, he is a contributor and organizer of *Startled Mediocre*, an Internet magazine.

Emily Doubilet lives in **New York City** and wrote "Auntie Jill's Clay" during her **freshman** year at **Trinity School**, also in the city. Emily participates in all Trinity drama productions and has worked professionally in an MTV-sponsored educational video for teens on conflict resolution and in *Safe Men*, an independent film. Also a dancer, she dances at the National Dance Institute and has twice performed at the White House. The daughter of underwater photographers, Emily says she "grew up laughing under the cool waters of the world" and that she goes scuba-diving as often as possible.

Nava Etshalom ("Summer Rain," "Archaeology, Circa 1892," "Letter to My Father") wrote her works in her **senior** year at **Masterman School** in **Philadelphia, Pennsylvania**. She lives in Philadelphia. A poet and fiction writer, Nava is also an avid reader and an enthusiastic traveler. She serves as a leader and counselor in her Jewish Socialist Youth Movement group and considers herself a political activist. Due to start her freshman year in college in the fall of 2000, Nava is taking this year off to seek adventure.

Sarah Fahey lives in Amesbury, Massachusetts, and attended **Phillips Exeter Academy** in **Exeter, New Hampshire**. She wrote "Separation" in her **senior** year. A varsity track team member, Sarah also captained Exeter's junior varsity soccer team and likes to bike and run in her spare time. Strong interest in politics led to her being elected vice president of the Democratic Club; concern for the environment inspires her to a biology major in college.

Stephanie Feldman lives and goes to school in **Philadelphia, Pennsylvania**, where she wrote "A Girl and Her Rock Star" while a **sophomore** at **Masterman School**. An avid reader and writer, she particularly enjoys Beat Generation writers like Jack Kerouac and is involved in her school newspaper and literary magazine. One of her favorite causes is Stand for Children, an advocacy group that raises awareness of child literacy and the importance of reading to children.

T. Devin Foxall is a student at **Oyster River High School** in **Durham, New Hampshire**, and a resident of Lee, New Hampshire. "Each Day Is Valentine's Day" was written during his **junior** year. Devin's journalistic reach extends to investigative reporting, humor writing, and "being an overzealous, autocratic high school newspaper editor." Pastimes include reading, trail running, hanging out with friends at the Yogurt Shop, and dreaming about winning a Pulitzer Prize.

Keleigh Friedrich wrote "Drew, Warrior Princess" during her **junior** year at **Oak Park High School** in her hometown of **Oak Park, California.** Another of her stories, "The Fat Man and Me," was published in the *Merlyn's Pen* Annual Edition, Volume I. Among Keleigh's favorite things are "warm days, languid nights, and the *Insurrectos* that I sit with in Mrs. Forman's AP English class." Keleigh has recently learned to drive and enjoys snowboarding.

Evan Grosshans wrote "Chance of a Lifetime" during his **junior** year at **Lawrence High School** in his hometown of **Lawrence, Kansas.** A "serious writer for only three years," Evan placed first for his poetry in the Kansas Voices contest and has been published in various anthologies. Theater and music come first in his life: he sings in a select a cappella choir and plays bass guitar in the school jazz band and percussion in its marching and concert bands. Theater experience has included many roles in school and community plays as well as membership in the International Thespian Society. In 1996, Evan achieved the rank of Eagle Scout.

Aarti Gupta attends **Clarkstown High School North** in her hometown of **New City, New York.** She wrote "The Glue Jar" while in the **eleventh** grade. Her favorite activity, she says, is reading— everything but horror, mystery, and romance. She also loves Japanese anime. While "claiming no skill in either sport," tennis and soccer are great fun for her: "Unfortunately, though, I usually don't have time for either."

Sam Hancock attends school in his hometown of **Fort Wayne, Indiana.** He wrote "The Gift of Life" during **freshman** year at **Canterbury School,** where his mom was his English teacher. A writer and poet from early childhood, Sam especially enjoys writing poetry. He works on the staff of his school literary magazine, *Mimesis,* and is assistant news editor of the school newspaper, *Untitled.* Other pastimes include playing the piano and soccer.

Jessica Hitch wrote "So Stupid" in the **eighth** grade at **Austin Academy,** in her hometown of **Garland, Texas**. Reading and writing occupy most of her leisure time, as well as playing with her dog, Shona. Participating in academic pentathlons (five-subject competitions) is also fun for her; one of her essays earned her a medal. About her so-called "stupid" protagonist, Jessica reports that Ashlee is actually a composite of many people.

Dan Kahn, of Plainfield, Vermont, is a student at U-**32 Junior/Senior High School** in **Montpelier, Vermont**. He wrote and submitted this story in the **ninth** grade. In addition to writing, Dan enjoys acting, playing classical piano, and reading fantasy. "The

Felicity Maker" is his first published piece. "Being published by Merlyn's Pen," he says, "is a terrific and unanticipated honor."

Coco Krumme lives in Berkeley, California, and wrote "Desert Trumpet" while a **sophomore** at **The Urban School of San Francisco.** Among her pastimes are acting, writing, and playing soccer. A saxophonist, she plays in  the school jazz band. Whenever possible, Coco likes to drive to the Sierras with her friends and go snowboarding.

Sameer Lakha lives in Oakland, New Jersey, and wrote "Fear of Airplanes" while in the **sixth** grade at **Saddle River Day School** in **Saddle River, New Jersey**. Sameer likes to act in plays, is a drummer in his school band, and a third-year piano student. Reading occupies most of his leisure time, with special appreciation for the sci-fi works of John Vornholt and Peter David.

Johanna Povirk-Zhoy wrote "Crossing the Street" while in the **sixth** grade and revised it in the seventh grade at **Conway Grammar School** in her hometown of **Conway, Massachusetts**. She currently attends Deerfield Academy in Deerfield, Massachusetts, where she is a freshman. Johanna reports that she greatly enjoys writing and drawing, "basically, things where I'm in control," and that her best times are had with friends. Other activities include soccer and track, listening to music, movie-viewing, and collecting unusual things, "like sand, and tacky flea-market finds."

Loraine Reitman lives and goes to school in **Annandale, Virginia.** She wrote "Virginia Mud" during her **junior** year at **Annandale High School.** "I took up writing in sixth grade out of boredom and restlessness," Loraine says. Eventually, she intends to pursue writing as her primary source of income. "To prepare, I am learning to cook from scratch and knit my own sweaters." Favorite writers include Percival Everett, Octavia Butler, Mercedes Lackey, Anne McCaffrey, Sylvia Plath, and Wally Lamb. Loraine is active in community service, plays percussion, and is on her school's literary magazine staff.

Joseph Reynolds wrote "Lucky" as a **tenth**-grade interview project and brought it to fuller, narrative life the following year. Currently a senior at **William Penn Charter School** in his hometown of **Philadelphia, Pennsylvania**, Joseph has been a top-ranking player in the United States Tennis Association. He also composes, arranges, and plays trumpet in a jazz ensemble. Another of his stories, "The Bridge," appeared in the *Merlyn's Pen* Annual Edition, Volume II.

Jacob Rosenstein wrote "A Summer of Regret" while a **sophomore** at **Westfield High School** in his hometown of **Westfield, New Jersey**. Jacob reports that his favorite subjects in school are math, computer programming, and chemistry. A cellist since the third grade, he recently was chosen to play in a regional orchestra. Jacob is also active in intramural baseball, soccer, and basketball leagues.

Rebecca Scott wrote "December 1773" while an **eighth**-grader at Montgomery Middle School in **Montgomery, New Jersey**. A resident of Belle Mead, New Jersey, Rebecca now attends **Montgomery High School**, where she enjoys competing on her school's Science League, Science Bowl, and Science Olympiad teams. Other activities include playing on the school's soccer team and on a traveling team in the spring, flute-playing (five years), and reading (Tom Clancy and James Herriot are favorites).

Jenny Smith lives in Lake Bluff, Illinois, and wrote "The East Pole," a memoir, during her **senior** year at **Lake Forest High School** in **Lake Forest, Illinois**. Currently a college student majoring in English, Jenny's interest in creative writing found wide expression in her high school newspaper, literary magazine, and yearbook, of which she was coeditor. High school days also included varsity volleyball and basketball.

Alex Taylor lives in Rosine, Kentucky, where he enjoys close contact with nature, "far from concrete." He wrote "The Pongee Stick" during his **junior** year at **Ohio County High School** in **Hartford, Kentucky**. Alex tries to write for at least an hour daily and is especially drawn to the work of Stephen King, H.P. Lovecraft, and Ray Bradbury. His musical choices include The Doors, Pink Floyd, and Black Sabbath. One of the world's "biggest pessimists," Alex offers: "Not only is the proverbial glass half-empty—it was never full in the first place!"

THE GIFT OF LIFE

BY SAM HANCOCK

I remember the Christmas I learned how to make babies. My sister showed me.

I am the youngest in a large family. When I was six, my elder sister Alice was engaged to a singularly charming man, Jonathan. With all due respect, Jonathan was perhaps not the prince that my parents had envisioned, and conversation between the two parties, my parents and Jonathan, was always somewhat tepid.

With Christmas approaching and my sister's fiancé occupying the same house as my parents, things had become undeniably frigid. Jonathan, being an unfortunately slow but resourceful chap, had managed to botch his last two attempts to gain favor in the eyes of my parents. My mother, being paranoid, had found his gift of expensive deodorant to be a veiled insult, and my father had not been amused by the ceramic talking frog that burped "hello" when one walked through the front door, doing little to soothe already frayed nerves. It was when Jonathan received the full brunt of my parents' wrath after engaging the family in a rousing game of slapjack during my father's nap time, days before Christmas, that it dawned on him that some very special gifts might be in order.

On the day before Christmas, I set out at a determined pace for the playground behind my school. I paused briefly to hurl a few missiles of snow at Mrs. Pratchett's windows and stopped for a second or two to press my nose against the glass of the Ben Franklin Store. They were still there, all right! The glorious family of bright-eyed baby hamsters in their metal cages.

When I arrived at the playground, a dozen or so of my first-grade buddies were seated placidly on the ground, chewing contentedly on the new-fallen snow. I warned Billy Wright to steer clear of the lemonade snow, to which he was getting dangerously close. The last time I was there, I had seen Billy consuming it in vast quantities. I don't care for lemonade so I had abstained, but a number of boys had thoroughly enjoyed it (prompting edicts against it from doctors and parents). I sat down and took a handful of clean, white snow and took a fair-sized bite.

One of my classmates across from me, Joe Corrigan, raised a soggy head and regarded me serenely.

"What do you want for Chrismiss?" he asked inquisitively.

"A hamsta," I replied, snow rolling down my chin.

"What's a hamsta?" Joe asked again.

"It's a animul."

"That's stupid," said Joe.

"But I like it," I responded, unruffled.

"That's dumb," he said.

The chap was really beginning to vex me. I regarded him for a moment.

"You're dumb," I concluded.

He ceased chewing.

"Yeah?"

The gauntlet had been thrown down. A deathly pall of silence fell over the crowd. Billy's mouth opened wide, lemonade snow dripping out.

I took a deep breath.

"Yeah."

I returned home soaked to the skin—to the immense pleasure of my parents. My second-eldest sister, Ellen, a formidable gymnast, had just roused herself from bed and was engaged in typical seventeen-year-old activities, like doing flips off the doghouse into the snow—to the general amusement of all five other siblings. I have little doubt that if lunch had not been called, Ellen would have handsprung from the top of the doghouse to the top of our house! As it was, my mother came outside to call us in to lunch, hysteria ensued, and my father herded us inside—with some indelicate words for Ellen and disgusted looks at my snowsuit.

It was approximately ten minutes into our lunchtime discussion when Mother introduced the subject of Christmas presents. When her line of questioning crossed

HUMOR

my path, I looked calmly at her and replied, "A hamsta."

A very ruffled Mother looked over the tops of her glasses. An animal was unusual.

"Well . . ." she replied after a moment of contemplation. I sensed that she was extremely tentative.

My father broke in.

"I'm not sure a hamster is the best idea."

I was confused.

My mother had found her gift of expensive deodorant to be a veiled insult, and my father had not been amused by his ceramic talking frog that burped "hello."

"Why?"

My father shot me a patronizing glare.

"They make messes and have babies."

Ellen, the science prodigy of our family, looked up from her plate of spaghetti to unleash a deep secret of biology.

"Not males," she proclaimed triumphantly.

A clump of spaghetti halted midway between my father's plate and mouth.

He slowly set it down and fixed my sister with a disdainful stare.

"I do not want animals in this house." The spaghetti resumed its journey.

Quite unfortunately, Jonathan had missed this last portion of the conversation and had proceeded to the bathroom, midcourse, having just learned that a hamster would be the ideal gift for me.

Christmas Day arrived and the entire family had packed into the living room for the traditional ripping open of presents. My father was relatively pleased with the gifts, and his demeanor remained jocular until the last present.

As he reached behind the tree for the red-and-white striped box, his face suddenly turned ashen. Stillness fell upon the group as he quietly rose with the rather large present in both hands, his eyes murderous.

About a dozen small air holes had been pricked in the wrapping paper.

"Who gave this present?" he asked calmly, but with a restrained rage.

Jonathan stood up, raising his hand and smiling demurely. He didn't seem to have noticed the deathly still.

Alice covered her face with her hands.

"Oh," my father said, smiling back like an adder. "Oh, *you* did."

"Yep," responded Jonathan.

Again came the teeth-clenched smile. I could have sworn that my father gave the box a rapid shake as he handed it to me.

Needless to say it was a hamster, and though it elicited a great deal of adoration from my sisters, my father was unamused. In fact, after I had opened my present on that particularly sober Christmas Day, I seem to remember my father, pipe in hand, admonishing my sister's intended by saying, "If it is a female and has babies . . ." The sentence was left curiously unfinished as my father threw a meaningful glance at the iron poker lying against the fireplace grate . . .

Jonathan replied that it was indeed male and that my father could reassure himself at his leisure.

I took this moment to inform the fiancé that I was rather troubled by the lack of potential offspring. Assuming an authoritative pose, I asked him what first step *he* would take in creating babies. He turned a delightful and rather curious shade of scarlet-purple. Ellen instantly picked up on my statement.

"Well, if you really want him to have babies . . ." she prompted with a devilish gleam in her eye.

"Yeah, yeah!" I replied, captivated by my sister's suggestion.

I warned Billy Wright to steer clear of the lemonade snow. Last week, Billy had been seen consuming it in vast quantities.

My father and mother both flashed warning signs that are often accompanied by "grounded for two weeks" or "no allowance for the rest of the year" in neon blinking lights, which Ellen either did not notice or, more likely, ignored.

"Well," she said, reaching her hand into the cage of my hamster, newly christened Fatty, "you have to shake them up really hard."

This amazing information was accompanied by an action that would have sent ASPCA workers scampering in the general direction of the Beaver Dam Police Department and might even have prompted paradrop by an army of Greenpeace activists. The effect was no less

I asked my sister's fiancé what first step *he* would take in creating babies. He turned a delightful shade of scarlet-purple.

spectacular than if she had placed the animal in a paint shaker.

Fatty was just as surprised as the rest of the family. His tongue hung loose from the corner of his mouth, his eyes bulging cross-eyed out of his head, his feet and paws running at triple speed, trying to escape the grip of my sister. After ten seconds of this torture, Ellen smiled sweetly at my parents, ceased the shaking, and returned a dazed and exhausted Fatty back to his cage.

While my parents were apparently overcome by a wave of revulsion by my sister's act, my siblings seemed to have found the performance wildly amusing. I too was impressed by the show and carried Fatty out of the living room.

Fatty remained imprisoned in my room that night, and when I awoke my thoughts flew to him. Flinging aside my bedcovers, I rushed to his cage. My wish had come true! The shaking had worked! For there was Fatty, joyously nursing approximately eighteen blind and hairless babies. I was so excited that I ran downstairs to proclaim the good news to my family.

I skidded to a halt in the doorway and cried out, "Fatty's had babies!"

Ellen squinted up sleepily. "Really funny."

My father looked as if he had just imbibed a particularly sour glass of lemonade.

"Sure he did. Now sit down and have breakfast." He must have been thinking that a "birds and the bees" talk was long overdue.

"No, I'm serious. Fatty really had kids!"

"It doesn't work that way," Ellen replied. "You see—"

My father obviously wished the discussion to be brief.

"Ah, thank you, Ellen."

My mother looked up as if in a trance. "How many?"

"Eighteen," I chirped.

A glass of orange juice plummeted to the floor as my father rocketed from his chair, coming to rest inches from my face.

"Eighteen?"

Jonathan slumped miserably in his chair.

"Yep!" was my triumphant response.

The entire family charged upstairs to behold the awesome sight.

Inside the cage were eighteen baby hamsters, just as I knew there would be. I shouted joyously to my sister, "Now I know how to get babies!"

My father shook his head at me, glared at my sister's fiancé, and stomped out of the room muttering something about a "messed-up kid when he gets older."

I was unaware of another freak of nature that is absolutely true: Mother hamsters have cannibalistic tendencies.

My father was overjoyed. ★

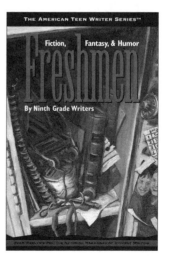

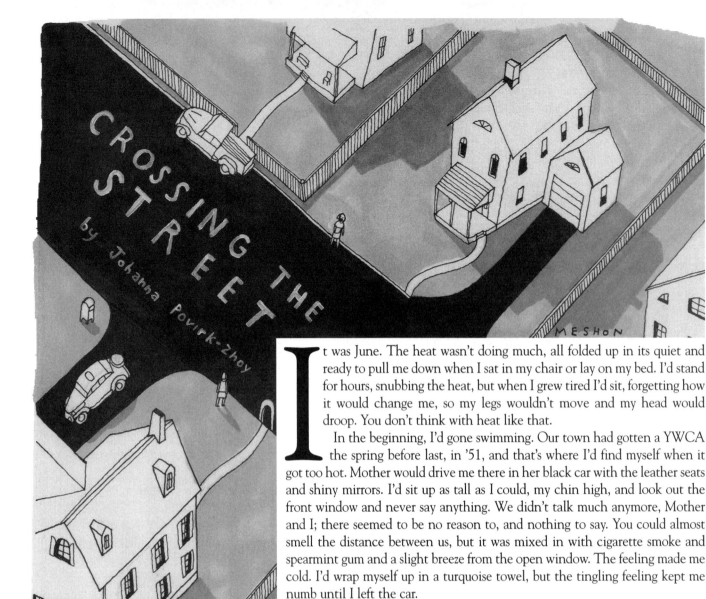

CROSSING THE STREET

by Johanna Povirk-Zhoy

By Johanna Povirk-Zhoy

contemporary
FICTION

It was June. The heat wasn't doing much, all folded up in its quiet and ready to pull me down when I sat in my chair or lay on my bed. I'd stand for hours, snubbing the heat, but when I grew tired I'd sit, forgetting how it would change me, so my legs wouldn't move and my head would droop. You don't think with heat like that.

In the beginning, I'd gone swimming. Our town had gotten a YWCA the spring before last, in '51, and that's where I'd find myself when it got too hot. Mother would drive me there in her black car with the leather seats and shiny mirrors. I'd sit up as tall as I could, my chin high, and look out the front window and never say anything. We didn't talk much anymore, Mother and I; there seemed to be no reason to, and nothing to say. You could almost smell the distance between us, but it was mixed in with cigarette smoke and spearmint gum and a slight breeze from the open window. The feeling made me cold. I'd wrap myself up in a turquoise towel, but the tingling feeling kept me numb until I left the car.

There isn't much to tell about the Y. It was just a place to go, a place with quiet hallways and a funny-smelling pool. Most of the time I practiced my diving. The other girls would sit, legs dangling, talking of whatever came to mind. I'd hear their conversations.

"No, she couldn't have done that! She just couldn't have . . . "

"But she did. That's . . . "

Then I'd be in the water going down, down, down, touching the bottom, and then up again, popping through the roof-like covering to hear their words again.

"No matter what, those were her exact words . . . "

Back in the water now, back to a world of quiet, then bursting out into noise. That was how it would go: in, out, in, out, and nothing could stop it. Then one of them spoke to me. Maybe she was tired of small talk, or sick of gossip. What I do know are her words.

"Margie," she said, half-laughing, "don't you ever talk?"

I kept walking toward the diving board, trying not to hear their curbed laughter. It pushed against my ribs, though, a hard pushing which moved up to my throat and made me feel stiff. *It isn't real,* I thought. *It just isn't real.*

That was a game I'd started during the summer. When something went wrong, it wasn't real. I wasn't Margie anymore, and nothing could hurt me. I tried to take myself away from my life. Everything was easier that way.

It isn't real, I thought again, and listened to my feet slap down on wet tiles. The noise was song-like, and I put words to it, not knowing where they came from. Each step was a word, repeating over and over in my head: *Don't cry. Don't cry. Don't cry. Don't cry.* I tried to concentrate on the pattern, but the laughter kept pressing. My game wasn't working.

"Margie."

It was the same one, and again she was talking to me. I glanced up quickly. A yellow bathing suit, brown hair; everything about her seemed to mix together with the rest of them.

"It's not Halloween yet. Why'd you go and paint your face orange?"

I dipped my face toward the floor so my hair would cover it.

Say something to her! I told myself. *Say something real mean.*

My mouth didn't move and my eyes followed my feet. I sucked in all my breath, wishing I weren't so shy.

"Cat got your tongue?"

It was another one this time. I recognized her voice as Peg from school. When I first started at that school, Peg was the one I wanted as a friend. She was always with someone, animated, popular, just who I wanted to be. I looked up quickly to where she sat. Her head was thrown back in laughter, and I knew I didn't want her as a friend anymore. She was just the same as the others, the five girls who sat around her, and the rest at school. They weren't real, all trying to impress each other and not one acting like herself.

"Ya' know, talking isn't so hard. I could teach you how," said another.

We didn't talk much anymore, Mother and I; there seemed to be no reason to, and nothing to say. You could almost smell the distance between us.

She sounded like she couldn't stop laughing. They all sounded like that, I guess. I wanted it to stop. I didn't want to be the one to stop them, and I didn't want to be laughed at.

The diving board was just a few steps away; only a little way and I'd be there. Peg began to speak again.

"Margie," she said in a singsong voice, "why don't you take off that horrible mask and show us your face?"

Everyone laughed, but I didn't care anymore. The diving board was rough under my feet, and I jumped off into the water. I went down as far as I could. Silence surrounded me on either side, but their words followed.

Mother picked me up a few hours later. She didn't seem to notice anything wrong, and I didn't tell her. My wet bathing suit was sticking to the seat, and I kept hear-

When something went wrong, it wasn't real. I wasn't Margie anymore and nothing could hurt me. Everything was easier that way.

ing Peg's voice: *Margie, Margie, Margie.* I twisted the towel viciously between my fingers, and wished it was a dream.

I didn't go back to the Y after that. The memory of their words was still boring an ugly hole into my stomach, and I didn't want it any bigger. Sometimes, I'd imagine myself going back and saying something to them, anything, to make myself seem big and brave. The dreams were nice but they died easily, and I stayed home, roaming the house and looking out windows.

That's how I first saw her, I guess. The window in the dining room looked out onto the street, and I was standing there when the car pulled up. It was a blue car, with fascinatingly fancy fenders and big headlights. I remembered something Father had said the night before about new neighbors, and realized this must be them. A small man got out of one side and opened the door for the girl. She was laughing and I let the yellow curtain I'd been holding fall into place. It didn't matter; she'd be just like the others, Peg and the rest of them sitting at the pool.

At dinner that night, Mother brought up our new neighbors.

"I baked cookies," she said softly. "I thought we might take them over."

I looked at my plate, shifting my fork up and down through the mashed potatoes. I didn't want to go.

"That sounds nice, Sarah," said Father. "We can go right after dinner."

Mother smiled quietly, and went back to slicing her meat. I watched as it was cut into small triangles, smaller and smaller, everything so exact and sharp. I knew she'd take a long time slicing and eating, too. Small and slow, that was Mother.

I looked back down at my plate, hoping dinner would last forever. I didn't want to meet anyone; I didn't want to go. Picking up my knife, I began slicing, slow and small.

As it ended up, I carried the cookie tin. It was Christmas-colored, and that embarrassed me, it being August and all. I studied the red and green plaid all the way across the street and up their stoop, too.

A man answered the door. I recognized him from the car, but I didn't say anything. Father was introducing us, throwing in a bit about new neighbors and friends. I let my mind drift away, hoping it would be over soon. The man asked us in, and I followed dutifully, grasping the cookie tin in my moist hands.

The room was warm. It was filled with boxes, and they seemed to push the heat at us as we came through the open door. I liked the feeling, in a way. It put me in mind of families, and ice cream, and laughter, and that was good.

A woman in a cotton dress walked toward us from amid the boxes. Her hair was pulled back, held in a dark clasp, and she looked tired, only in a good way. I smiled at her, deciding it was best to, and she smiled back.

"Lucy," she yelled into a doorway. "Lucy, come here. We have company."

I heard footsteps and in came the girl I'd seen before. She looked happy and good, and suddenly I wanted to be her friend. I didn't care that I was terribly shy, or that I'd never had a friend before. I just cared about meeting her, and I wanted that real bad.

After I'd gotten rid of the cookies, the grownups sent us upstairs together. I kept looking at my feet, wondering what to say and what she was thinking about me. It was hard, because I'd never met anyone this way before, where all I wanted was to be their friend. I followed her up the

stairs and then into a room which I guessed was hers. It was full of boxes, just like downstairs, but there was also a bed and dresser and pictures of movie stars on the walls. She got up on the bed, sitting cross-legged, and I did the same.

"Where do you live?" she asked, and I told her. Silence then. I looked down at my hands folded neatly in my lap and studied the nails. They were chewed and breaking. In my mind I tried to put them in order from longest to shortest. Left thumbnail, right . . . It was stupid,

"Margie," she said in a singsong voice, "why don't you take off that horrible mask and show us your face?" Everyone laughed but I didn't care anymore.

and I thrust my hands under my legs, hoping she wouldn't notice how anxious I was. I dug my nail into my leg, wanting to speak more than anything.

"You know, my last house was an apartment, so this place seems especially large," she said, and I looked up, scared but knowing I had to speak.

"Yeah," I said. "My Aunt Judy's house is out in the country, a really old place with these huge rooms. Whenever I go there I feel, well, more open."

She looked at me then, and I put my head down, feeling like I'd said something dumb. *Stupid, stupid Margie*, I thought, digging my nails into my leg once more. I hoped I'd pierce myself, I hoped I'd draw blood, I hoped . . .

"Yeah," she said. "I feel the same way."

We talked then, she mostly leading the way and me fumbling around like a newly blind man finding his way up the steps. I can't remember what we said—talk of her friends and the city she'd come from, my relatives, and books I'd read. After a while, the steps became stronger and the blindness dwindled to a mere haze. When Mother came up, I was leaning against the wall beside Lucy's bed, laughing at something she'd said. Mother came in timidly, and I looked away from her, wishing she wouldn't stand all crumpled like that.

"Margie," she said, smiling politely at Lucy, "it's time to go."

"Just a minute."

I slid off the bed, awkwardly grabbing up my shoes. Mother stayed in the doorway, that senseless smile still on her. I tied my laces wishing she'd leave, just so Lucy and I could get in a little more talk, and a real goodbye. Standing up, I brushed back my hair and looked at Lucy.

Night Life

You love the summer night,
the way its warm breezes
blow against your face,

the scared feeling you get
when you look deep into the dark trees
no longer peacefully green, but mysteriously black.

You thrill in racing through the night
while the bright stars glimmer above,
like silver marbles on display.

You see the headlights chasing away dark shadows,
the windows down all the way
and the dark sky pouring in.

—*Alex Brabbee,*
Seventh grade, Micos School,
St. Louis, Missouri

She was pretty, I thought, not typical, but pretty. I walked toward Mother and then turned back, resting my foot on the opposite heel.

"Goodbye, Lucy," I whispered, and she smiled. That was where it all began.

"Margie, where'd you get your name?"

We were lying on the floor, poring over old issues of *Photoplay*. I was studying Jane Russell's profile when Lucy spoke.

"I'm not sure. Something about a great-grandmother Margaret," I said, making a slight face. "How about yours?"

"It's a bit of a mix," she said slowly, and I scooted over to her side to get a better look at an Esther Williams photo.

"How?" I looked up when she didn't continue.

"Well, I'm named after Joan Crawford *and* Lucille Ball," she answered, stretching the names till they filled the room. "But more for Joan Crawford, I think."

I was quiet, waiting for the story.

"Her real name," said Lucy, "is Lucille Fay LeSueur. Mom was just crazy about her when I was born, but they couldn't name me Joan because of a cousin and Mom's sister. They didn't want to get the family all mixed up."

She took a breath then, and I turned to lie on my back.

"Anyway, Mom did a bit of research and found out about her real name. Dad thought it was fine, because he was a Lucille Ball fan and all, so they named me Lucy, Lucille really, but Lucy all the same."

I smiled and took a sip of my soda.

The thing about Lucy was she always had stories. I liked listening to them, and the way she told them was like life was going to last forever, and there was nothing to worry about. In the beginning, I was half-jealous because I didn't think I had stories. I guess they were hidden, down inside in a place where I had to pull and grasp to get them out. I learned that, after a while, and soon the pulling wasn't needed—stories just came. I thank Lucy for that.

We did more than talk, though. We'd go to the movies, walk down shaded streets, and bike when the heat wasn't too overwhelming. Even when we were doing something other than just talking, the words were still there. They'd hang over us as we'd laugh over a dress, or cry at Bette Davis's last line. I remember once we walked down the street, completely quiet, but it didn't matter because we both knew the words were there; we could just pull them right down. Lucy looked at me and smiled.

"I was just thinking," she said. "You're not like my other friends who act like silence is some sort of monster. I mean, we're comfortable together, aren't we?"

I nodded because I knew it was true. Yes, the words were always there, making that summer one long song of friendship.

I loved her family, too. It was small, like mine, but it managed to hold a sort of warmth that in my house always escaped through the cracks in our walls.

Mrs. Randolph was pleasant-looking, with light hair. She worked on Tuesdays and Thursdays as a bookkeeper.

Lucy looked happy and good. Suddenly I wanted to be her friend. I didn't care that I was terribly shy, or that I'd never had a friend before.

It was strange for me to think of her in some office balancing accounts, while my mother stood by a sink scrubbing pots and listening to the daytime soap operas.

Mr. Randolph was a small man who came home every day at 5:30 sharp. He wore a tan suit and always asked about my day. I liked that part. It made me feel noticed and important, like I was more than just his daughter's friend.

Some days, when Lucy and I were at the table eating lunch, her parents would sit down, too. They'd talk to us as though we were like them, and it made me swell with

Who Am I?

The trees ask me,
And the sky,
And the sea asks me
    Who am I?

The grass asks me,
And the sand,
And the rocks ask me
    Who am I?

The wind tells me
At nightfall,
And the rain tells me
    Someone small.

Someone small
Someone small
But a piece
    Of it all.

—Taylor Nikolaus,
Sixth grade, Briarwood Elementary School,
Renton, Washington

pride. It was all so different from my house, where politics were discussed behind closed doors and grown-up conversations ended when I entered the room. Here I heard about the world beyond my home, and it interested me. Rights of Negroes. Labor unions. Strikes. Often what they said was opposite of what I'd been taught, but it made sense to me, because their words all sounded so fair.

On most Saturdays, Mr. and Mrs. Randolph would

"You're not like my other friends who act like silence is some sort of monster. I mean, we're comfortable together, aren't we?"

leave the house in the late afternoon. I asked Lucy about it once, and she said they went to meetings. I didn't ask any more questions.

They were different from us, I thought, different from my family. I could tell it was somewhere lurking in the pages of the books with long titles on their shelves, something that wouldn't fit with Mother's *Reader's Digest* condensed books. It was mixed in with the swirling paint of the art in their living room, something that didn't match our grainy family portraits. It had to do with strange newspapers and friends who would come to lunch and talk, and a house that wasn't ruled by what a magazine ad said it should look like. They had different thoughts than

Mother and Father regarding just about everything, it seemed. The strange thing was, when I was there I felt like I was home.

Lucy's family was close, the way mine used to be. Sometimes I didn't believe we'd ever been like that, what with our silence. I'd walk across the street toward home, and my quiet, lonely self returned. I'd put my hands into my pockets and bend my head. Automatically, my feet would slow and my hair would form a curtain in front of my face.

Inside, the house was quiet. Mother sat at the dining room table sewing, getting up occasionally to check the potatoes. Father would be reading the paper, sometimes talking to himself. I'd sit on my bed and wish it wasn't like that.

Mother and I were becoming more and more distant. We'd talk at dinner, but it was always the type of conversation you could have with a stranger.

"Are you going to Lucy's again tomorrow?"

She knew the answer, but would ask anyway.

"Yes, Mother."

The quiet that followed was horrible, heavy, and pushed me back against my chair. I tried to act like it didn't matter, but that was impossible. Silence would just flood over us until Father said something about work, and we could move on.

Father tried to make us family. He would talk when there were no words, and always managed to smile and pat me on the back. Before Mother and I had drifted apart, we

had been family. Father wanted that again; I could hear it in his voice. He tried so hard, and it made me feel guilty when the quiet filled the room, hurting him more than me.

He was a patriotic man, against Communists, the whole bit. Some days he'd inform Mother about all the political happenings, and I'd overhear. Though I'd listen, I just didn't care. Because, really, my life was Lucy now.

Then the rumors started.

It was the type of hot day when the thought of wool sweaters or beef stew made you feel sick and dry. The weatherman had said it was ninety degrees, but we knew it was more. I was lying on my back and sipping a Coke. Lucy was doing the same. The heat had trapped us so it was impossible to move, and when she spoke, the words seemed to stick in the air.

"Margie."

My name filtered through the heat to my ears.

"Margie, we *have* to go swimming today, we just *have* to!"

I'd told her about the Y, of course, and the other girls. She understood all that, I knew, and the truth was they didn't matter much anymore. I still hurt from it, but the feelings were losing their strength, and I knew I could face them again. Easily, too.

So Lucy and I went to the Y. We walked the whole way, laughing and talking, just like usual. By the time we reached the yellow brick building, the need for a swim was great. We raced through the hall, changing its quiet into a flood of noise with our pounding feet. Already a trace of chlorine was following us, sticking onto our sweaty bodies and enveloping us in a heavy smell. We got to the changing room and pulled on our bathing suits, wet tiles underfoot. Then we were in the pool area letting our toes play in the pool's gutter.

To a Tigress in a Zoo

Tigress, why your amber eye
must gleam with grief? I think I know
what stimulates your heartfelt pain
to manifest—fortissimo.

And as your bellow fades to naught
I sense your silent rage;
I feel your fettered soul lash out
beyond the bars of your cruel cage.

—Sarah Moore,
Ninth grade, James I. O'Neill High School,
West Point, New York

The girls were there. We both noticed them right away. Lucy gave me a look, and I nodded, telling her these were the ones. We walked over by them, and Peg stopped us.

"Who are you?" she asked Lucy in a voice that had made a decision already.

Lucy gave a little smile and spoke.

Rights of Negroes. Labor unions. Strikes. Here I heard about the world beyond my home —and it interested me!

"My name is Lucille Fay LeSueur," she said, slurring the last word until they were all looking at her.

I looked down at my feet, but this time it wasn't in shame. I slapped my foot down on the tile floor to keep myself from laughing. Lucy was going on.

"I love to have dances," she said, and I could see her looking down, too. "Once I had quite a large one, and a friend came up to me and said, 'Lucille, what a ball!'"

We both cracked up then, at the same time, as if it had been planned. They were looking at us, taken aback, trying to understand. Lucy was on the floor now, she couldn't control it, and I felt the laughter pushing at my sides.

Peg was tapping her foot. She gave a sort of sneer in our direction, then opened her mouth but didn't say anything.

"It really is Lucille," said Lucy from the floor, "but most people call me Lucy."

We couldn't look at each other anymore without laughing.

A voice came from their group.

"You're the new girl, then," she said. "The one who lives on Lindwood Street."

Lucy nodded, and looked a bit worried.

"Yeah," she said slowly. "What about it?"

"My father says your parents are commies, and your dad writes for some sort of Red newspaper."

Gift

Breathless,
the pull of a ribbon,
silk soothes the moment.

—Lisa Dicker,
Seventh grade, Lewis F. Cole Middle School,
Fort Lee, New Jersey

Lucy took a deep swallow and looked up at me.

"My dad said the same thing." This came from Peg. "He said your father is running from the government, and your mother does anything to support the commies."

I looked back down at Lucy, and knew what I had to do.

My feet slipped a bit as I walked toward Peg. She had her head tilted back in a defiant way, and I found myself looking to the side, away from her. My head was spinning and my stomach hurt. Peg's blue bathing suit seemed to mix in with the tiles behind her, and I spoke.

"Leave her alone," I said loudly. "Just leave her alone!"

Peg tossed her wet hair back, spattering my face.

"And who are you to tell me what to do?" she said, voice thick and sure. "Who are you to talk to me like that?"

"I'm her friend, that's who."

Nobody said anything, and Lucy got up.

"Let's go," she said.

I turned around then, walking near the wall where the sticky wet faded away. Lucy followed in the gutter, water splashing in rhythm. I joined her, and our feet created a hard tune of continuous sound. I wondered what they thought, what they wanted to say. It didn't really matter, though, because before long we were gone.

Later, on the way back, she told me.

"You know, what they said was true."

I gave my dress a tug, rubbing my toe on the back of my leg awkwardly. I'd known it, of course, from the way she looked when the girls were talking. I'd known it, but hearing it was harder. I thought about Father and the way he spoke about Communists, as if they were all terrible. I let my mind sit there for a while, and then made it move

"I don't want you seeing Lucy anymore. Her parents are Communists. You understand, of course, that I don't want my little girl growing up with a Communist."

on to Lucy and her family. They were people; they were good. I remembered the way I was treated over there, like I was an equal, and it made me smile a bit. I thought about her, I thought about my friend.

"It doesn't matter," I said calmly.

She smiled.

"Good, Margie," she said. "I'm glad."

We talked about it then, and I heard how her heart would race in school when something came up, something that had to do with it all. I heard about why they'd moved, how there'd been people watching her house, and I heard about the fear.

A couple of weeks later I knew that Father had found out, though he hadn't said anything direct.

"Tomorrow you're not going to Lucy's," he said as I passed the butter.

"But I always go! I mean, she'll be expecting me."

Father glanced up from his bread, toward Mother.

"Your mother and I feel we need more time as a family," he said firmly.

She looked up, a bit confused, but nodded all the same.

"Yes, dear, we thought perhaps . . . "

Mother never finished her sentence, and Father spoke up as soon as she began to trail.

"The truth is, we feel you're spending too much time with Lucy."

I shrugged. "She's my friend."

He opened his mouth but seemed to change his mind.

"Yes, well, tomorrow you won't go over there. All right? Tomorrow we'll go for a drive or to lunch or something."

"OK," I said, because I knew it had to be.

We ended up going to Sunset, the diner near Father's office. The place had a glow that mirrored from the

counter and the glass of the jukebox and the grease. When I was little, we'd gone there a lot, and Mother would fix my hair into two braids. She loved my hair and would always brush it, telling me it was just like hers when she was little. We had traditions around it: braids to Sunset, high ponytail to Grandma's. And I loved the feel of her fingers gently pulling out the knots.

Father asked me questions about Lucy all through lunch.

"What are her parents like, Margie? How do they treat you?"

"Real nice." I bit off the end of a French fry.

"What do they talk about . . . her parents, you know, Lucy's parents . . . ?"

I looked up and squeezed the soft potato out of its skin. It got on my finger.

"Stuff." I licked my thumb.

"What kind of stuff, honey?"

He knew, I was sure of that, and it scared me. He could take me away from Lucy now, maybe he could do it forever. I picked at the bottom of my hamburger, determined not to give Lucy's family away.

"You know, stuff."

I watched the table in front of me and saw his hands pound down on it, sending his face close to mine.

"Margie!"

"I don't know!"

I tried to look helpless, and Mother pulled his arm back.

"Andrew, now . . . " Her hand was still on his shoulder.

His shoulder shook her hand off, and he jerked it into her lap, then picked up a French fry with a fork.

"Well then, Margie, what kinds of magazines do they read? What sorts of books do you see over there?" Again, his face was close.

"I don't know. *Look. Lucy* has *Photoplay*."

He made a grunt and took a bite of his hamburger.

"OK, honey. I was just curious," he said, the meat visible in his open mouth.

I felt disgusted. This man was my father, but he questioned me like a criminal. I took a bite of my sandwich, and the feeling I felt about the man across from me made it taste sour.

At least he wasn't positive, I thought that night alone in my room. Fear hung over me like a weighted canopy, pressing on my head and holding it down. *At least he wasn't positive*, I thought again. But that did nothing to penetrate the cold and foreboding.

I thought he'd forgotten, until a week later. Now he was sure of himself.

"Margie," he said, in a nearly strict voice, "I don't

want you seeing Lucy anymore."

I looked up from my plate, anger and surprise taking over.

"What do you mean?" I asked, and when he didn't answer, "You can't be serious!"

He put his fork down and looked at me with a calm, sympathetic stare.

"I know this is somewhat sudden," he said slowly, just to make sure I understood, "but her parents are Communists. Margie, you understand, of course, that I don't want my little girl growing up with a Communist."

My head felt funny. I wanted to say something, but he was already back to eating, and I started to slide down in my chair. I didn't want this. I couldn't have this. How could he take away Lucy? I began to drift, to try to make it unreal, and then Mother spoke.

"Andrew," she said, rushing the words, "Andrew, Margie'd never had a friend until Lucy, and Lucy's just the kind I wished she'd have." She stopped, coughing. "And her family, it's good. I talk to her mother sometimes, and she's decent, Andrew, she's real decent. Her father too, though I don't know him as well. What they believe doesn't matter; it's who they are."

She stopped, and I didn't know how to feel. Mostly surprised, I guess, but there was something else—something I couldn't name. Later, I knew it was pride. I felt it for myself and for my friendship, but mostly I felt it for my mother. She'd stood up for me and understood. I felt our distance shatter with her words.

Later, when I crossed the street to Lucy's, there was no change from quiet to alive. I was one person now. ★

Moonlight

Last night I pattered through
the kitchen
through the living room
past the bedroom and closet
and into my room where I
spied a patch of white glowing floor.
I knelt down
and my fingers brushed the
smooth surface.
It was moonlight and it
lit the room.

—*Luisa Colón,*
Seventh grade, The Center School,
New York, New York

By Rebecca Scott

historical
FICTION

Mother was sick that autumn of 1773. The illness betook her not so poorly as it had my late father, but it prevented her from going out as much and slowed her sewing in our small tailoring business. Consequently, our income fell, and I took up more of the work. In December her health took yet another turn for the worse, so that the morning of the 16th found me hurrying to the apothecary before a delivery.

After I had bid Samuel Stanley, the apothecary's apprentice, farewell, I tripped down the street, trying to keep my basket from being jostled. Excitement sparkled everywhere: in the shop windows (one merchant's window was boarded over, shattered by angry patriots); in the clop of horses' hooves through rippling puddles; in the mist of rain that blanketed the air; in the hustle of the people themselves. Something was about, I knew, but as to what, I was as well-informed as the neighbour's dog. My ignorance was mostly my mother's doing. If I ever chanced to make mention of something I'd heard in the street, she'd lash out immediately with a harsh scolding. Politics, she admonished, was not the business of women. We were to attend to the home, to the cooking, to the sewing in the shop.

Perhaps it was cleverness that kept Mother out of the politics and goings-on. It was impossible for a Boston man to walk a middle road in these times, choosing to side neither with the Tories nor the rebels. A widowed woman, however, with no husband to choose sides for her, could accomplish this—and Mother did. We had both Tory and patriot patrons; neither group could find fault with an innocent widow. Thus, we were not much threatened, physically or economically, by the turbulent times.

Or perhaps her ignorance was a result of her distaste for the mob that had, essentially, caused my father's death three years before. In 1770 we had been living in Boston for but a year, moved there recently that my father might receive the attention of a doctor. He was sickly and could not handle the rough labour that farm life demanded. It was an icy March night when my bedridden father grew suddenly worse. I stayed with him, I remember, while Mother slipped out to fetch the doctor 'round. Father coughed in long, wrenching sounds; his breath came in terrible wheezes. When Mother returned hours later, doctorless, the laboured breath had ceased. A jumble of people milling in the streets and surrounding the Customs House had hindered my mother's search for medical help;

the clogged streets were practically impassable and no doctor was home. Even the apothecary had disappeared in the throng of angry people. My mother was under the conviction that a doctor could have saved my father. And since the mob had prevented her from finding a doctor, it had killed him. I was but nine at the time, and rather cloudy as to current happenings; but ever since, Mother had tried to instill in me a hatred of mob action. Her own views were neutral toward both sides, against only the friction between the groups. I, however, could not remain so unswaying. Vaguely, I blamed the Bostonians—those unintelligent hotheads—for my father's death. They were unruly. They had disobeyed the law, gone against the wishes of the royal King George III. The power to rule belonged undeniably to Parliament, to England—did it not? What nerve had they, I wondered, dodging a little scamp of a boy, to defy this unchallengeable authority?

For they had been challenging the king all these years. They had boycotted imports, harassed soldiers, held meetings. They were evidently up to something again, and a broadside posted on a shop door confirmed this:

FRIENDS! BRETHREN! COUNTRYMEN!—THAT WORST OF PLAGUES, THE DETESTED TEA, SHIPPED FOR THIS PORT BY THE EAST INDIA COMPANY, IS NOW ARRIVED IN THIS HARBOUR—THE HOUR OF DESTRUCTION OR MANLY OPPOSITION TO THE MACHINATIONS OF TYRANNY STARE YOU IN THE FACE. EVERY FRIEND TO HIS COUNTRY, TO HIMSELF, AND POSTERITY, IS NOW CALLED UPON TO MEET AT FANEUIL HALL, AT NINE O'CLOCK THIS DAY, AT WHICH TIME THE BELLS WILL RING, TO MAKE AN UNITED AND SUCCESSFUL RESISTANCE TO THIS LAST, WORST, AND MOST DESTRUCTIVE MEASURE OF ADMINISTRATION.[1]

I hurried on once I had skimmed the paper, mindful that Mother would not approve of my taking notice of such. So it was the tea that was causing all this! From odd gossip on the street and conversation among patrons of the shop, I had heard a little of the tea ships, the first of which had arrived in harbour on the 28th of November. Gossip had failed to inform me, however, how three ships carrying loads of tea could create such a stir.

I shuffled on down the busy street. People were beginning to gather around Faneuil Hall in response to the broadsides, pacing about expectantly. The large group around the Hall—so big, I doubted they all would fit inside—looked docile enough, but hard feelings could bring any sort of eruption.

Let there be no violence, I prayed, dashing across King Street. *Let there be no mob!* From then on, however, my thoughts were heavy with making my way through the streets to New South Meeting. It was a fair piece, and I was becoming only slowly accustomed to the winding city streets. There was so much to see that I grew distracted, and continued too far on Newbury Street. Retracing my steps by way of Essex Street and Blind Lane, I was rather over-whelmed when I reached New South Meeting.

The church was empty, it being Thursday, but for a tall lad sweeping the floor by the pulpit. His broom whisked briskly against the floorboards, muffling the sound of my footsteps in the big building. It was this lad—Ben Howard—whom I sought. He was studying the ministry with the reverend, and his duties, as well as assisting the minister, included cleaning the church.

"Morning, Edith," he greeted me brightly, leaning his broom against the pulpit. "What's brought you 'round?"

I set down my basket and took from it the shirt I'd finished hemming the day before. "I've finished your new shirt."

Ben skirted the pews and strode down the aisle, whistling softly as was his habit. "So you have. Right good, it looks. I'll be sure to wear it come Sunday."

I handed it to him. "Mind you don't spill on it during the Sunday dinner."

"I shan't wear it tonight," he mused.

I WAS AS WELL-INFORMED AS THE NEIGHBOUR'S DOG. POLITICS WAS NOT THE BUSINESS OF WOMEN.

He paused for a moment, apparently mulling something over. Something of his manner inspired me to inquire, "Have you seen the broadsides?"

"Aye, indeed. Looks like we don't plan to drink our tea sitting down, do we?"

"'Twould be better if they didn't cause a commotion. No need to create such a stir over nothing."

"'Tis the principle of it, Edith," Ben said gravely, no longer whistling.

"Principle?" I scoffed—perhaps just to make Ben explain.

"You know how we've been boycotting the East India Company's tea, do you not?" he began. "Well, consequent to that and other matters, they were suffering, and had an alarming surplus sitting there in England. They couldn't afford to pay the duty to land it for sale there, so our beloved Lord North set his mind not to charge them that tax in England. He's had them send the tea here, so that he might force *us* to pay his tax. Threepence duty a pound, indeed!"

"A pittance," I murmured.

"As I said, Edith, 'tis the principle of it. What gives them the right to force us to buy their tea—and pay their taxes?"

"*Isn't* it their right, though? They are, after all, the royal British government."

"But who *gave* them that right? They go against their own *Magna Carta!* They said themselves, so long ago, that one shouldn't be taxed without representation!"

"That was long ago. It's practically a different government now! To go against England must be treason! The rightful government—"

"That's just it, Edith," he said, his voice softening, becoming wistful. "What makes the English government the rightful power? What dictates who is in the right? What makes their law the authority? Forget not that even England was the object of many struggles for power. So

I BLAMED THE BOSTONIANS—THOSE UNINTELLIGENT HOTHEADS—FOR MY FATHER'S DEATH. THEY HAD GONE AGAINST THE WISHES OF OUR ROYAL KING GEORGE III.

should we say that the British rule is the rightful one?" Ben waited for me to say something; then, seeing that I would not, added, "In short, what is it that decides England to be the rightful government? Who says that our campaigns and arguments are illegitimate?"

I stood, dumbfounded, as the words ran 'round my head, much like a dog chasing its tail, so far they got me. For so long, I had assumed Mother England the rightful ruler, the correct power. Ben's words had the effect of turning my thoughts upside down and giving them a brisk shake. Confused, I lunged for my basket and lifted it abruptly.

"Thank you for the shirt," Ben said. He seemed to understand my confusion, even take pleasure in it. "I appreciate the trouble you took in delivering it."

I curtsied, mumbled, "It was no trouble," and wheeled

around. The reverend was standing in the doorway, evidently witness to the scene just transpired. He stepped aside so that I might pass, but as I was stepping through the door back into the bustle of the street, he said, "Edith?"

I glanced over my shoulder at him. "I do not know what God would think of all this." He gestured 'round, as if to suggest not only the mayhem with the tea, but all the colonies' struggle with Mother England. "The Bible says to honour thy mother and thy father. So the loyalists argue, and the rebels combat them with other evidence from the Holy Book. I do know—take note of this, Edith Hunter—that civilizations rise and fall, governments come in and go out of power. Only the law of God will survive forever."

"Thank you, sir," I said, bobbing another curtsy. Then I hopped down the steps and scurried into the street, pondering these new thoughts as I walked.

When I arrived home, Mother was worse. I found her asleep in her bed, cheeks flushed with fever and sweat beading her forehead.

Leaving my basket by her darning table, I eased myself down on the bed and pressed the back of my hand against her cheek. Burning hot, she was. I dipped a rag into the washbowl and held it against her face. Mother's eyes fluttered open and she reached for my hand. "The . . . cool cloth feels nice," she stammered weakly.

"How are you feeling?" I asked, trying to conceal my desperation.

"Weak," Mother acknowledged. "Tired . . . weak. Hot . . . and cold. Do poke the fire, please."

I stood up, strode to the fireplace, and tossed a log on top of the smouldering ashes. Seeing that bigger flames were beginning to leap, I returned to Mother's side. "Mayhap I should call for the doctor."

"No, Edith, my good girl, not yet. Get me . . . another damp cloth and . . . go to the other room. Work on the sewing."

"Yes, ma'am," I obeyed, wringing a rag over the washbowl and applying it to her forehead. I took my basket to the other room and sewed absently on a pair of breeches. *Who made England the rightful power?*

By midmorning, I had made little progress on the breeches and Mother's fever seemed to have grown worse. Ignoring her pleas to stay and work on the sewing, I slipped on my cloak and went to fetch the doctor. When he arrived back with me, he examined Mother briefly, grunting dismally, then bled her. His work was shortly done, and I walked him outside, taking care to shut Mother's door so she could not hear us.

"Is there nothing more you can do?" I asked.

"Nothing. Just keep with the cool cloths, make certain she is comfortable. With the grace of God, she'll recover."

I shut the door after him, feeling more uncertain than

before he'd come.

The afternoon was long, long and tedious. I took my sewing to the bedside so as to work while I watched Mother. And to think. I could not get Ben's words out of my mind. *What made England the lawful government?* Occasionally I opened the window and ducked my head outside. The distant gong of bells drifted to my ear. The view of the buildings was the same as it always was, but an excitement pervading the atmosphere made the air inside the room even more stifling when I drew in my head and shut the window with a clang.

In the late afternoon I cut myself some bread and meat, which I tried to eat as I kept vigil over Mother, but the sickroom was so stuffy I could not stomach it. Mother grew no better, and discouragement welled within me. This was quenched by relief when a rap on the door reverberated through the house. I bolted from the room to answer it and found at the door our neighbour, Mrs. Dayton.

"How is your mother?" she inquired, placing in my arms a pot of soup "for the sick one."

"Much worse. The doctor was about but he offered no help."

"Let me watch her for an hour. You look as if you could use a breath of fresh air."

"Thank you, ma'am," I said, afraid that hesitation or a polite refusal would cause the offer to be withdrawn. Grabbing my cloak, I hurried down the steps into the night, which had fallen in the past half-hour. It was about quarter of six, but dusk came early to December days.

The night air was cool, and the little gusts blowing up the street felt good against my face. The street was quieter than usual. Normally at this time of night, the city has taken on a second life, men striding briskly home from work, unruly lads dashing back from the wharves to supper.

The wharves. I would go there. The smell of salt air from an abandoned dock would clear my head. Speeding my gait as I approached Blind Lane, I prepared to cross the road and continue down Summer Street. I had just passed the Lane residence when someone bumped me from behind.

"In a hurry, are you?"

I was about to retort in annoyance when I turned around and saw the spectacle who had bumped me. He was half a head taller than I, so I stared not quite directly into his twinkling eyes. His face was black, coal black. It glistened in the light of the lantern that he gripped in his left hand. If I had not been thus startled, I might have seen in

FRIENDS! BRETHREN! COUNTRYMEN! THE WORST OF PLAGUES, THE DETESTED TEA, IS NOW ARRIVED IN THIS HARBOUR . . .

him a faint resemblance to an Indian Mohawk, but in the flickering of the lantern light he appeared merely odd. And frightening. Oh, how gruesome it all seemed!

"I do beg your pardon, miss," he began, his familiar voice courteous. "I hope I have not caused you a scare."

"Indeed not," I said pertly, regaining my composure. Before he could duck away I swiped my finger across his face; a thick black film coated my digit when I drew it back.

"Lampblack," I muttered.

"Doesn't stay on the face too well," said the form, walking away. "I didn't want to risk getting any on my new shirt tonight."

I watched as he hurried away, turning the corner onto Purchase Street.

Something was happening, no doubt. Something with the tea. *Will they do something unlawful?* I wondered. *Something against the king? Or—mayhap they are preparing to do something righteous. Righteous in their own idea of the law.*

I had been headed for Bull's Wharf, but instead I trailed Ben's path down Purchase. The tea was tied up at Griffin's Wharf; I'd go there.

The road became busier as I tramped along, crowded with streams of people heading for the wharf. Voices rose from around me, audible over the sound of raucous yelling and boatswains' whistles.

"They denied the boat captain, Roch, clearance to leave the harbour . . ."

"Meeting broke up a little while ago . . ."

"Heard Adams say . . . 'This meeting can do nothing more to save the country.'"

"We'll turn the harbour black, we will . . ."

"Let the English sip some saltwater brew . . ."

I was on the wharf now, scuttling on the wooden planks for a view of the water and the tea ships. My view was severely obstructed by tall shoulders, and no manner of maneuvering could win me a glimpse of the harbour. Fighting my way back, I made up my mind to go to Wheelwright's Wharf and try to see from there.

Wheelwright's Wharf was a ways from the tea ships. I could see their masts poking up toward the stars, one out-

"TAKE NOTE OF THIS, EDITH HUNTER: CIVILIZATIONS RISE AND FALL, GOVERNMENTS COME AND GO. ONLY THE LAW OF GOD WILL SURVIVE FOREVER."

lined against a full yellow moon which cast light on the harbour. I watched three smaller boats, oars propelling them steadily against the waves toward the ships. Their occupants' faces were black as the dark water they skimmed, and an occasional whoop rode a cold ocean gust to my ear. I watched as the men scurried aboard each ship; I saw one confer with a ship's captain. Then I saw crates and crates appear from the holds, and the gleam of ax blades breaking them open. I watched as men hoisted them to the sides of the ship, letting the tea fall into the water as if it were slop into a hog's trough. I heard some shouts, but there was nothing of the pandemonium that had penetrated the walls that March night my father died. This was different, somehow, from riot; other than the excitement of tea brewing in the harbour, there was peace.

They're going against the law, I reminded myself. *They are going against the King!*

Somehow the bite of those words had dissipated. *Is there anything to make their doings any less righteous than the King's?* I countered myself, recalling Ben's line of thought.

Glancing up at the moon again, I minded that it was late. I must be getting home to relieve Mrs. Dayton and watch over Mother.

Mrs. Dayton greeted me at the door upon my arrival and was promptly gone, eager as I had been earlier, to leave the sickroom behind. I hung my cloak on a hook and made my way to Mother's room, easing myself into a chair beside her.

By and by, Mother roused herself. I inquired as to how she was getting on, but she showed no interest in talking of her health.

"Tell me . . . where you were," she demanded weakly. So I did.

". . . and they're there yet, tossing the tea into the harbour," I concluded.

"Unlawful . . . going against England," Mother murmured.

"Righteous by their own law," I defied her, seizing Ben's

philosophy as my own. "And who says theirs is any less legitimate than England's?"

Mother did not say anything. She closed her eyes and seemed to have fallen asleep. Moments later she opened her mouth and drew a deep breath, startling me. "You may be right."

Indeed, my own doubts had now vanished. There was no way of telling for certain which side—the colonies or England—was in the right. The colonies, backed by a handful of polished ideals, were now challenging the empire of Britain, which had behind it the grounding of a thousand years. Neither side could be proven the correct one; as the reverend said, the only lasting and righteous government was God's.

I did know, however, that the defenders of those polished ideals had taken the liberty tonight to dump thousands of pounds of tea into the water. And, as Mr. Franklin says, "God helps those who help themselves." I prayed that night, as Mother fell into a calm sleep, that God would fall on *our* side in our quest for righteous—if only temporary—government. ★

[1] Lukes, Bonnie L., *The American Revolution*. Lucent Books, 1996, p. 51.

My Pet

The firebellied toad
I bought at Petco
sits in my palm like a tiny
puddle of cold water.
His skin puckers like a pickle
and shines in the fluorescent light.
I drop a cricket
from an empty cottage cheese container
into his terrarium.
His eyes rotate,
following the insect over unfamiliar terrain.
Like a cat, he creeps
between branches of plastic ivy
toward the camouflaged cricket,
hunches, then leans forward.
Suddenly his gummy tongue lashes out
and wraps around the prey.
Legs twitch, and the cricket-lump
disappears into the toad's mouth
and down his throat into a tiger-striped
belly where I can see it throb.
My pet deflates into his clear
Tupperware bath.

—Claire Anderson,
*Twelfth grade, Mead High School,
Spokane, Washington*

Chance Of A Lifetime

By Evan Grosshans

[Lights up on two Friends, neutrally dressed, facing an ordinary Boy; an ordinary Girl stands off to their left]

FRIEND #1: You know, she really likes you.

FRIEND #2: You should talk to her.

BOY: You really think so?

FRIEND #1: What have you got to lose?

BOY: Yeah. I mean, why not?

FRIEND #2: She's had bad relationships before.

FRIEND #1: But we know you won't burn her.

FRIEND #2: Because you're a nice guy.

FRIEND #1: One of the reasons she really likes you.

FRIEND #2: You should talk to her.

BOY: What have I got to lose, right?

FRIEND #1: You never know.

FRIEND #2: This could be what you've been wanting.

BOY: Come on. This is high school. I'm not even alive yet. How could this be what I want—what I *need?* So soon?

FRIEND #1: You never know.

FRIEND #2: And you *need* to know what you want.

BOY: What if I don't ever want to know? Why can't it just happen? What happened to chemistry? Love at first sight? Seeing a stranger across a crowded room?

FRIEND #2: People aren't always what they seem.

FRIEND #1: People change.

FRIEND #2: Feelings can betray you.

FRIEND #1: Feelings change.

BOY: But I can't make them change, can I? I can't make myself feel, or love! That's not true love!

FRIEND #2: What is truth?

FRIEND #1: Would you know true love?

FRIEND #2: A room can be crowded with three people in it.

FRIEND #1: She really likes you.

FRIEND #2: Give it a chance.

FRIEND #1: Relationships are what you make of them.

FRIEND #2: You don't know how the story ends yet.

BOY: But I've read this book a thousand times! Sure, it's a different title, a different author, but the plot never changes. Just the characters. And the length.

FRIEND #2: You don't know how *this* story ends yet.

BOY: Oh?

FRIEND #1: You can't contain life in a book.

BOY: Why not?

FRIEND #2: Because books only come in black and white.

BOY: Not all of them.

FRIEND #1: They are two-dimensional facsimiles of life.

FRIEND #2: The equivalent of black and white replacing color.

BOY: It's art! Art imitates life!

FRIEND #1: Not real life.

BOY: Or does life imitate art?

FRIEND #2: You should talk to her.

FRIEND #1: Walk with her.

FRIEND #2: Listen to her.

FRIEND #1: Maybe you'll see something to like.

BOY: Not love?

FRIEND #1: What have you got to lose?

DRAMA

BOY: What if I get in too deep, though? If I don't love her, don't want to spend the rest of my life with her, why should I know her dreams and ambitions? Her deepest fears? Her joys?

FRIEND #1: You never know.

BOY: Why do I have to *know*?

FRIEND #2: Do you know what you feel?

BOY: *[He faces the Girl]* I want to know. If it's something other than nothing, I need help to find it.

FRIEND #1: She can help you.

FRIEND #2: Love conquers all.

BOY: But this isn't love. This is "like."

FRIEND #2: "Like" conquers much.

BOY: This is nothing!

FRIEND #2: It could become something.

BOY: *[Unwillingly takes a step toward the Girl and starts to take another]* How long will that take?

FRIEND #1: Relationships are what you make of them.

BOY: *[Stops in mid-stride]* I don't think I have enough time to make something out of nothing. I still have to live, live my own life.

FRIEND #1: Stop and smell the roses.

FRIEND #2: You should talk to her.

FRIEND #1: Walk with her.

BOY: *[Starts walking again, very slowly, very deliberately]* What have I got to lose, right?

FRIEND #1: Don't let her go.

BOY: *[Stops abruptly]* So now I've made a commitment, is that it? I took the first step and now I've got to see it through hell and back?

FRIEND #2: That's how you play the game.

BOY: But who makes the rules? Whose game is it?

FRIEND #1: No one knows.

BOY: I never even wanted to play. Who wins? And how?

FRIEND #2: Why do you have to *know*?

BOY: *[Prepares to take another step]* Yeah, right.

FRIEND #1: She really likes you.

BOY: *[Stops again]* What if she's wrong, though? About me? What if she's mistaken me for someone who cares?

FRIEND #2: If you didn't care—

FRIEND #1: —why would she like you?

BOY: What if I don't care about *her*?

FRIEND #2: If you didn't care—

BOY: But what if she's wrong?

FRIEND #1: You never know.

BOY: *[Takes another step]* And why do I have to know?

FRIEND #2: Right.

[The Boy takes another step]

FRIEND #1: Walk with her.

[Another step]

FRIEND #2: Talk to her.

[Another step]

BOY: And love?

FRIEND #1: Relationships are what you make of them.

BOY: And love?

FRIEND #1: You know, she really likes you.

BOY: Sure. I get it. Why do you have to *know*?

[He reaches out to the Girl's arm, and she turns to him]

Hi. Do you—?

GIRL: Yes.

BOY: How did you—?

[He takes a deep breath and starts to begin again, but she interrupts him]

GIRL: Why do you have to know?

[They stare at each other; after a moment, she takes his hand]

Walk with me.

[Blackout, as the Friends watch them walk slowly upstage into a setting sun] ★

FIRE AND WATER

By Jim Cady

contemporary FICTION

y sister is going to hell; at least, that's what Brother Jimmy on Channel 19 would say. This is because she is an atheist. I feel like I should at least do something to help her, so the other day when we came home from school I said, "Audrey, you are going to hell."

Audrey looked at me in disgust.

"There is no hell. Who's been feeding you that line of crap?" I was too embarrassed to tell her I saw it on TV, so I shook my head and let the subject drop. Another thing my sister doesn't believe in is truth. Talk about crazy! She says she's a *nihilist* and "accepts the absence of truth in the human condition." This is why kids at school call my sister a freak. Everyone knows there's truth—even me.

For instance, it is true that my name is Jude and that I'm a boy and that I'm eleven years old. I also know that I am not from this ugly little town. My mom told me I was born in Montana. All these things are true, so how can there be no truth? Something else that's true: Montana is very, very far away from Lecompte, Louisiana, which is where I live. If you watch the Discovery Channel like I do, you know that Montana is the "Last Frontier of the American Wilderness." This means it has lots of trees and bears and stuff. Lecompte has no trees. It also has no bears, but the neighbor's dog looks kind of like a wolf. My dad says he'll shoot it if it gets into our garbage again.

Dad works for Exxon. Usually, he works offshore, which means he is gone for a long time. It's while he's gone that me and Audrey get into fights about God. Nobody fights while my dad is around; he doesn't take any crap.

Last Thanksgiving, when my cousins were visiting from Georgia, my dad kicked my sister out of the house. What happened was, my sister and my cousin Jamie got into the wine coolers and beer while Dad wasn't looking. When he came downstairs for Thanksgiving dinner, Audrey threw up on the table and Jamie fell out of his chair, laughing and hiccuping. The whole room got quiet. I looked around the table; my mom and Aunt Martha and Uncle Harvey and my cousins Reid and Janna were all looking at my dad. He stood up and looked taller than he ever had before. I thought he looked like one of the police guys on "Cops," the ones who break up the fights. He pointed to Audrey and Jamie and said, "Out."

My mom tried once: "Terry, please—"

"Shut up. Audrey Marie Cabot, stand up. Stand up! You will leave this home—right now."

The silence was hurting my ears. My sister, still drunk, I guess, started to cry. Mom lit a cigarette and stood up.

"Come on, Martha. Let's get this table cleaned up." She was shaking all over and her face was red.

My dad just stood there, the muscles in his jaw jumping up and down. And my sister left; she came home two

My sister says she's a *nihilist* who "accepts the absence of truth in the human condition." This is why everyone calls her a freak.

days later when Dad was back at work, and she's only said about two words to him since then.

My sister says she stopped believing in God a long time ago, way before the Thanksgiving Incident (as my mother calls it). But I think that's when it happened. Or maybe she just forgot about God. I'm not sure, though. How do you forget about God and heaven and hell? Is it all at once, like a light bulb switching off in your head, or does it take a long time? Can a person just forget? I ask Audrey this, and she tells me, "It's not about belief. You just open your eyes." Yeah, some answer.

Being worried about Audrey going to hell made me think about God, and what I still know for sure. I don't always know what's real anymore. I mean, when you're little, you believe in stuff like Santa Claus and the Easter Bunny. But then you figure out that it's not true. So what *is* true? Is hell true? What's it like? I do know about heaven— I even know what it's going to be like. Heaven is like swimming. See, swimming used to be my and Audrey's favorite thing in the world. That was a long time ago, back when we lived in Georgia, back when my sister and I were buddies (that's what she used to call me: her buddy). We'd spend all day at the pool, swimming circles, holding our breath, doing

Unexpressed

What is more tragic
than the tragic personality
which lives a tragic life,
suffers a tragic mind,
and yet, in experiencing its tragedy,
can only express it
in words not even its own?

—Jay Menefee,
Eleventh grade, Kenston High School,
Chagrin Falls, Ohio

dives, lying on our bellies on the warm concrete. Finally we'd ride our bikes home, our eyes cloudy and stinging from the chlorine. The cool weight of the water and that endless blue quiet—that's what heaven feels like. Except there, you can float forever, and you never have to come up for air.

Now we don't live near a pool and Audrey is too old to be my buddy, and I'm kind of forgetting what heaven felt like anyway. It seems like the more you know, the less you're sure of.

The last time my father came home from work he was a day late and he didn't bring his whole paycheck. I know this because my mother asked him and his eyes got that warning look, like "Don't push it." I think that after dinner she did push it because I heard them arguing. The air conditioner's droning was covering it, but when it shut off, the sound of shouting came bursting through their door. They must have realized that the air was off, because suddenly there was silence. When I heard the muffled, angry voices start up again I snuck into Audrey's room. Audrey was by the window, and her room was thick with smoke. Not cigarette smoke like Mom's, but that stronger, earth-smelly smoke I always smell around her friends. This told me she too had heard the swearing through the door.

My sister looked up at me but acted like she didn't even see me. Then she said, softly, "It's so stupid and clichéd— right out of a B movie. We're regular trailer-trash Bradys." I started to tell her that our house is way better than a trailer, but I picked up that she was being sarcastic, so I just stood there. Sarcastic people aren't really being funny— they just don't want to be serious. I think it would've been cool if I had stayed there and we had comforted each other and promised to stay together forever, like orphans on TV. But we both know that we don't need comforting just because of a little shouting; we're used to it. So I left a *How to Be Saved* pamphlet in her room, hoping she would read it and remember God. Then I went to bed, and that night I had no dreams.

At my elementary school, we have P.E. every other day. On Wednesdays, we play flag football. I hate flag football because Danny Broussard always tackles me "by accident." So I stayed home sick the next day. My sister stayed home too, but I don't know why. She doesn't even have P.E., so why stay home? But you never can tell why my sister does things, so I forgot about it and started watching TV. In the morning there are no good shows on, mostly kiddie stuff like "Mister Rogers' Neighborhood." But by the time Audrey woke up, the talk shows were on. We sat on the floor together and watched a man who'd married his daughter by mistake, and then some cross-dressing senior citizens. After the commercial, a man came on who likes to burn the American flag. I changed the channel and Audrey got mad.

"Hey! Change it back."

"Why?"

" 'Cause I was watching that."

"Aud, I don't want to watch that guy. He's some kind of freak or something."

She sat up and narrowed her eyes, and I knew she wanted to argue. "And just what makes him such a freak, Jude?" Teenagers are so weird.

"He's burning the American flag! That seems pretty darn sick to me."

"Yeah, well, that flag happens to be a symbol of tyranny and lies! Do you know what this country is founded on? Do you? God, don't they teach you kids any history?"

"Yes, they do too. George Washington founded this country, and Christopher Columbus discovered it. In 1492. So there." I wanted to stick my tongue out at her, but that would have been immature.

"Starting with Columbus, explorers here were all guilty of exploiting and killing the natives, raping the land, and destroying our natural—" I changed the channel, but Audrey did not stop yelling—"ecosystems! This nation was built by trespassers, thieves, and greedy, killing politicians. Look at the Vietnam War! Look at our President now, and the one before him, and the one before him! We're being screwed over, and most people couldn't be happier! Waving their little flags around—their little banners of oppression! What is wrong with you people?"

"Geez, sorry, Audrey. Man!" I tried to interrupt her. She faltered and stopped, slamming her fist on the floor. Now she spoke softly, sadly.

"You don't get it, do you? You believe everything they've told you. Poor baby." I still can't believe she had the guts to call me a baby after a tantrum like that. She really is a freak. I couldn't believe Mom was going to be leaving me alone with her.

See, Mom had just told us that she was going to take a Greyhound to Aunt Martha's house for the weekend. They hadn't seen each other since Thanksgiving, and Mom really needed to get away, she said. Dad had just left and would be gone a few weeks. So while Mom was gone, Audrey'd be in charge. Last time that happened, Audrey's friends came over to spend the night, and they were pretty wild. It was horrible, except that her friend Natalie, who is really pretty, talked to me and played Sega with me. The other ones were all stupid—they talked through me as if I was a little kid. They stayed up all night, and I was surprised Mom never found out about all the stuff they did. I was even more surprised that Mom was leaving her in charge again. But that's Mom for you; she's kind of weird sometimes. Like forgetful, or spacey. I remember once she left a roast in the oven, and the oven almost burned up. So I guess her leaving Audrey in control isn't as strange as it seems.

I came home from school Friday all set to watch TV. I got off the bus just like I always do and walked down the patchy blacktop road. Most of the houses on my street are trailers, with old rusting cars on cinder blocks in the yards. There are no trees in my neighborhood, except for a pecan tree in the LeBlancs' yard. Most of its branches have been cut off and painted over with that white gunk, and it looks like a tree from a horror movie. Our house is the one with the peeling white paint and the broken porch swing; Mom keeps saying she's going to fix that swing, but she never will. I stomped up the creaky steps, and I could already hear music.

The living room was empty, but I could hear my sister's friends in the back—they must have left school early. The night would be long and noisy; I could tell from all the party stuff on the table—plastic cups, two-liter Cokes, bags of chips. I went straight to my room, wondering if Natalie would come over. My room has a tiny portable TV but it doesn't get cable. "Wild Discovery" would be coming on soon, and I knew that the party people wouldn't be watching it. So I had to drag the heavy TV from the living room all the way to my room. I got it inside and slammed the door just as my sister's pierced and tattooed friends were heading for the living room.

When Dad came downstairs for his Thanksgiving dinner, Audrey threw up all over the table and Jamie fell out of his chair, laughing and hiccuping.

On "Happy Days," when the gang has a party, they play records and do the twist and eat hamburgers. My sister's parties are not like that at all. The music is loud and angry and they all sit on the floor, yelling and smoking and passing around guitars. If it was summer they'd be outside on skateboards, but now that the weather was cooler, they stayed inside, messing up our house. When I came out during a commercial, I caught sight of a boy and a girl under the table. Together. Sometimes Audrey's friends really gross me out.

Safely back in my room, I turned to a Western and settled down. By the end of the second movie and an infomercial about a new food processor, it seemed quieter outside. I guess even freaks and atheists can't stay up forever. Between shows, I went out and snuck a peek. Most of the people had left. Audrey, Natalie, and some boy were all asleep on the floor. The house was trashed, as usual, and an overflowing and smoking ashtray was lying near my sister's hand. I took a good long look. You know, when my sister is asleep she reminds me of how she used to be, back when we were buddies and everything was simpler. I guess I'm just fooling myself, but it seems like when you're little everything is perfect. I don't remember things like Mom and Dad yelling at each other, living in a crummy neighborhood, or Audrey being brought home by the police all the time. But we are still the same people, so I couldn't resist pulling an old flannel sheet over the pile of bodies that was my sister and her friends. I can still see the smoke curling up from that ashtray, and reminding myself to clean it up in the morning. Doing something nice for them made me feel good, and I went right to sleep.

In my dream, I was really cold. I had been swimming, but the water dried up all of a sudden. I was resting on the bottom of the pool, except it turned into our kitchen. And my mom was saying, "Oh, no, I forgot the roast! How could I be so stupid? It's on fire!" I could smell it too, charring and smoking, choking me. And then Audrey's voice, more like a shriek, cut into my dream. I opened my eyes, still smelling the roast. Everything was thick and smoky, making my eyes water. I decided I must still be dreaming, and rolled over. I'm not sure when I realized what was happening; was it in the split second when I shut my eyes again, or was it when Audrey came screaming into my room? All I know is, the feeling you get from a fire is like nothing I had ever felt in my life. I mean, I've seen "Rescue 911," so I knew I wasn't supposed to panic, but—it's so *scary*. Standing there and watching your sofa leap with flame, like some crazy plant; fire shooting out from all different places, the heat sizzling my bangs and singeing my eyebrows. I'd never felt so scared as when I watched the lump of melting plastic Coke bottle bubble on the floor. I remember thinking, *Where's Audrey? What happened to Audrey? Oh my God, where is my sister?* Then I felt someone grab me from behind, and whoever it was dragged me through the door. When I finally collapsed in the yard, it was Audrey who fell on top of me.

When I came to, there was a boy leaning over Natalie, crying. What was making this teenage boy cry? I mean, it wasn't *his* house that was burning up. Natalie's flannel shirt was open all the way down, but that's not what made my stomach lock up. It was the reddish-brown, leathery skin that covered her shoulders and neck, the cracked-looking white blister welts that stood out on her back. Somewhere in my head I knew that this was really, really bad. *This is not television. This is true,* I kept telling myself.

Then the words broke out of me like sobs, and I was sort of chanting them out loud: "This is not TV, this is not TV, this is not—"

It was Audrey who held my head, cradled in her arms. It was Audrey who turned it sideways when I threw up. When I was finished, my stomach still heaved and churned. I rolled my eyes upward and saw the smoke pouring from our house, like from the smokestack at the Lecompte Paper Mill. I closed my eyes and sank back onto my sister, where I fell asleep.

We've joined the YMCA in Baton Rouge, so every Tuesday and Thursday we go down there and swim. I can dive off the middle-high dive now, not the highest one but the one beneath it. Audrey can dive off the highest, but I can still hold my breath longer than she can.

How do you forget about God and heaven and hell? Is it all at once, like a light bulb switching off, or does it take a long time?

Our new house is actually a trailer, but it's on the outskirts of Baton Rouge and not in Lecompte. It's close enough to my new school that I can ride my bike there.

Audrey's friend Natalie comes over every now and then with her new boyfriend. The burns don't look too bad anymore, but you can tell where they are because they don't tan.

Dad still works for Exxon, and he still doesn't take any crap from anyone. But he laughs when he calls me "Smokey" or "Firebug." And Audrey talks to him sometimes—at least when she wants money for gas. And Audrey—well, Audrey is the same old Aud. Her hair is blue right now, and she still thinks that God is not real. She still makes fun of the American flag.

I would have liked my sister to have been converted by the experience of our house burning down, for her to have "seen the light," as they say. It happens on "The 700 Club" all the time. But even I know that life is not always like TV. And what's on TV is not always the truth. But I'm not all that hooked on TV anymore. Every Tuesday and Thursday I meet Rosalyn Andrews at the pool, and we swim together. When I'm underwater in that cool blue quiet and I open my eyes to see a cloudy, watery picture of Rosalyn, I never want to come up for air again. I tell my sister this, and she says, "It's about time, Jude. I was beginning to think you'd never come around." Teenagers can be such freaks. ★

Shorts

Each Day Is Valentine's Day
by T. Devin Foxall

Today was one sexy day in the middle of an already steamy year for the Devman. That really hot girl in the office? Well, she talked to me. I mean, *talked* to me. I was by the coffee machine, just hangin' and puttin' out the vibe, when she sauntered by. I played it cool and produced a little extra vibing action just for her. No one else was nearby. *Good,* I thought, *a little privacy.*

"Do you know what time it is?" Her eyes looked deep into mine, searching for answers.

"Sure do." I was playin' it cool. Playin' a little hard to get. Makin' her work for it.

"Could you tell me?" She was no actress, and I could see love seeping through her mask of annoyance.

"Twelve," I let the suspense build, "thirty."

Without thanking me, she uttered a sigh and walked feistily down the hall.

Meow!

I whipped out my pocket mirror. Not a hair out of place, muscles in full view under sleeveless shirt, eyes like Leonardo. Stud factor: 10. So it was no surprise that my day of love was far from over. Cupid had ammo left, and he'd traded in his bow for a stun gun!

Just then, one of the curvy vice president babes told me to report to her office *immediately* to deal with "issues of incompetence." Yeah, I read ya. A lady in the adjoining cubicle asked me for a pen. I saw right through her plan. "Isn't that a pen right there on your desk, you cunning little vixen?"

"That's a pencil. I need a *pen*." Gotcha, baby! The Foxall satellites have picked up your call for love. Houston, we have an admirer.

Of course, my appeal doesn't fall off outside of the office. I skipped the last ten minutes of work so I could beat the end-of-the-day rush to my car. With a dollar to burn I headed for Brooks, home of the $.99 ginseng tea. The cashier was particularly sassy. "Have a nice day," she

whispered. I stared at her for a few extra seconds.

"Keep the change, baby!" She seemed paralyzed by my gaze and began tapping something under the counter. I've been in this situation before; she obviously felt overwhelmed and outclassed. That's OK, dollface. I'm like fine wine: only enjoyed by a discerning few.

My last stop was the deli. I walked slow and cool to the take-a-number machine. I took a number, then gave some serious thought to taking the machine. It would have come in handy—help the ladies line up in a more orderly fashion.

The heat of the chase forced me to cruise home with windows down. Heading into the setting sun, I knew that my encounters with love were far from over. The plush seats of my spacious Volvo wagon were empty now but would soon be filled with ladies, like clowns in a circus car. Summer was rising to action. ★

Fear of Airplanes
by Sameer Lakha

The fear that any second one of these passengers could jump up and yell "This is a hijack!" and someone would get shot and the cabin be filled with screams and smoke, to heck with security because anything's possible these days, or maybe an explosion just comes out of nowhere and the 757 is blown to pieces so high that there's no oxygen and the temperature's well below zero or maybe a bit lower, and I get sucked out of what's left, still belted to my seat, and technical difficulty at 15,000 feet or lower spells JUMP OUT AND HOPE YOU LAND IN A MEADOW but over water it's LIFE JACKETS ON AND SLIDE OUT WHEN WE SPLASH DOWN AND JUST HOPE THE WATER IS SAFE, and speaking of slides, you take a 757 and those emergency slides open in midair and WHOOSH, nice knowing you! but if you're a bit lower and you end up actually using them, and if fuel is leaking from the rear, you can wish all you want that you took that Atacama Desert Heat Survival Course, wish and wish again, but you're still toast when the fuel hits the jet exhaust, and then I wish they wouldn't show that darned safety video before takeoff which freaks me out so much my sweat rusts the seat-belt buckle and I go deaf because I forget to swallow while thinking about how we all die, maybe 'cause I'm in the aisle when the plane hits a storm and I crack my head on that bar service cart, or the cabin pressure suddenly drops while I'm at the other end of the plane using the bathroom, and my oxygen mask malfunctions . . . Oh, God! There's SO MUCH TO FEAR ON A PLANE! ★

Summer Rain
by Nava Etshalom

Summer rain, the cold-on-hot, backwards-hot-fudge kind, that falls in driving winds from the sky, erodes the edges of California and never touches Israel, sends up waves of pavement-scent in New York and earth-scent in Idaho and brushes your mountain with tears that cut holes in your cheeks and expose your bones to the wind. You dance in it, your hair falls even longer down your back, reaches for the ground; your white shirt has given up all pretense of modesty and your bra-lines are nonexistent this summer. You are still eleven. You push out your skirt, looking for hips, wiggling your waist in the air and

shedding drops like cat fur for the sun to clean up. Running down the drain in swirls and yowls, the cat fur is a foreshadowing. Like Nair, the rain drives your leg hair from your skin to clog the sewers. Razors call you a teenager and introduce you to a self-absorption that is contained within walls of glass-shards-in-cement to keep everyone out. You try to climb out but your skirt and legs are torn; a rip sears up your leg and your crotch is dripping blood. You cry but don't feel clean, think you'll never feel clean again. Your thoughts are dirty, your holes are dirty, and you're still dirty behind the ears. Your fingers are dirty and sticky from the rain and your tears aren't freshwater; they're the salt of a syrupy dead sea. ★

[Other works by Nava Etshalom appear on pages 9 and 85.]

A Summer of Regret
by Jacob Rosenstein

Deep in the Pocono Mountains, the small circle of poorly built cabins followed Karl's lead and awoke without a sound, their shadows drawn into hiding by the rising of the sun. It was early enough that birdsong was the only noise breaking the silence to welcome the new day; in less than an hour the spell would be broken by the chattering of waking teens. For the moment, however, the serenity of early morning reigned.

A small, barely noticeable creaking sound accompanied the birds as Karl quietly jumped down from the top bunk, put on his shoes, and left the cabin, his mind filled with thoughts that he had yet to understand. So many things had happened since he arrived at camp at the beginning of the month, and the cramped cabin, smelling of sawdust and sweat socks, was no place to decipher them. Karl felt that he needed to be alone—to get some time to think, unbothered by his fellow campers.

Silent as the air around him, Karl left the cabins' vicinity and allowed the image of a girl he had admired all month—though he had yet to learn her name—to enter his mind: long, flowing, chestnut-colored hair; beautiful figure, and—

"Ow!" Karl hit the ground with a thud as he slipped on flat, moss-covered rocks that he hadn't seen. He brushed himself off and hurried past the sports field, where he had not found the courage to approach her during the Independence Day Dance. He passed the dining hall, where, three times a day, she had been directly in his line of sight as he chewed the pig swill that just barely passed for food. Next along the path was the adventure-training shack, home to camping supplies and memories of her as she walked, just paces ahead of him, with their hiking group.

In fact, not a day had gone by that she was not in Karl's view, just beyond his invisibly outstretched arms. But not once had he been able to overcome his fear of rejection, the pessimistic expectation that was always foremost in his mind. Her "stranger status" tormented him, yet there was no way to solve the problem other than by the obvious approach that Karl had so far failed to try.

He quickened his pace along the well-worn path, the pitter-patter of morning showers in sync with his footsteps. Soon he would reach his destination, the place where nobody would be at this hour, the one area that would be utterly silent.

The lake at daybreak was an intense royal blue, rimmed by majestic pines. Their long reflections shimmered on the crystal-clear water, and the mass of liquid seemed to possess a luminescence of its own as Karl neared it, though he did not notice: early morning weariness and his single-minded focus were a blindfold to the world.

There she was! Nothing could have surprised Karl more than seeing her at that moment. Fewer than ten yards separated them, though only one person was aware of it. More than once had he imagined that they would cross paths on this sunrise expedition, though these were only fleeting notions. Never had he seriously expected *this* to happen . . . but there she was!

The gray boulder that she was sitting on must have reposed at the water's edge for thousands of years, and Karl felt that this time must have at least been matched in the few seconds that he stood, paralyzed by the angelic being who was only a few strides away. Images of lost opportunities flashed through his mind as he remembered the purpose of his early rising. The solution to all of his problems was right there in front of him!

Karl moved slowly across the vacant lakefront, at last summoning the courage to risk failure. The awaiting girl seemed to give off a radiance all her own as he approached, and the birds' songs were reduced to whispers as a young man sought to reverse a summer full of regret. For just a moment, the melody stopped entirely, as one small word passed meekly through Karl's lips: "Hi." Startled at first, she turned around and smiled—and voiced the same simple greeting, "Hi."

A faint whistle broke the silence, and within seconds, the Pennsylvania woods were filled with song again. ★

So Stupid
by Jessica Hitch

She continued her struggle, racing after the object of her desire and constantly reminding herself, *Stalking bad, stalking bad. Just be calm, not obsessive! No, scratch that— just talk for once!* Ashlee darted around a cluster of seventh-graders and continued diligently, chasing her crush. Focusing intently on her beloved one, she zeroed in on his feet, his beautiful feet, which were nearing the end of the hall and which were also the only part of him she could see through the boisterous crowd. *Look at those shoes— they are so cute! And blue is my favorite color! Hold on! He's getting away!* Ashlee went into panic mode and began

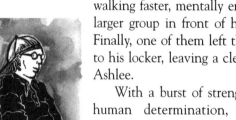

walking faster, mentally encouraging the larger group in front of her to disperse. Finally, one of them left the group to go to his locker, leaving a clear opening for Ashlee.

With a burst of strength and superhuman determination, she swerved around the group, only to crash into her science teacher, mash some guy's foot, and, to the sound of the guy screaming in pain, whack someone in the stomach with her overstuffed backpack. Ashlee cringed at her path of destruction, but didn't stop to apologize. For there was no time today on this, her day of destiny.

Today will not only be the day that I approach Seth, but also actually talk to him! Today is going to be my Independence Day! No, Ashlee! she immediately screamed in her head. *That's exactly why he thinks you're so stupid! You're way too cheesy! He'll just laugh at you, or kick you, or something!* Ashlee shook her head and pressed on, now much less confident than before. But there was no way she could turn back now—just a few feet from his adorable spiked hair and enchanting green eyes.

Suddenly he stopped in his tracks and turned around,

as if he'd forgotten something, and Ashlee was left standing right behind him with her mouth wide open. At first, she couldn't bring herself to look at his face and instead stared at his shoes; but then, having no other choice, she took the plunge.

"Hi!" she blurted. As soon as the too-loud word was out, she scolded herself. *'Hi!'* she mocked. *That ranks up there with 'I think you're cute.' Ugh! So stupid, so unbelievably stupid!*

"Hi, Ashlee!" he replied happily, interrupting her thoughts. Ashlee nearly melted. *He knows my name! And he's happy to see me! Uh . . . hold on! Seth has red hair, not brown! How could I not have noticed? I am soooo stupid! It's not him!* Ashlee's cheeks flushed a deep crimson as she spun around and ran in the other direction, somehow managing to trip over the same science teacher (who was still picking up his papers) and to swan-dive along the dusty floor. Totally embarrassed, she jumped up and gathered the textbooks which had gone flying during her fall. As if that weren't bad enough, she suddenly noticed that her "I ♥ Seth," scribbled on the inside cover of her history book, was now on full display. Defeated and humiliated, she ran recklessly down the hall, finally reaching the double doors at the end and bursting out of the school of horrors.

Seth just stared after her, open-mouthed. *Dang!* he thought as he smoothed his newly dyed hair. *Talk to her next time!* ★

Auntie Jill's Clay
by Emily Doubilet

My dad's sister, Auntie Jill, was an artist. I remember going to her studio, where I spent the whole day with cool brown clay oozing through my fingers and under my fingernails. The cold, mushy stuff felt good against my palms. I sat at a steel table in which I could see a cloudy reflection of myself, blotched with clay. I simply sat there, grinning into the dim reflection as my fingers massaged the soft material for hours. Eventually, I started rolling the clay into long thin cylinders. They felt smooth and strong, yet were so fragile and delicate that I could squish them with a pound of my fist. I placed them on top of one another and made a

coil pot. Auntie Jill offered to bake the pot for me, turning the tender clay rock-hard, but I wouldn't hear of it. I liked it smooth and soft.

"That's the way I like it too, Sophia," she spoke with a dreamy haze in her eyes. Flecks of gold glinted in her deep brown eyes as she peered over her crooked nose at me. Tears welled along the red rims of her eyes. Her bony, clay-stained hands trembled as she spoke, barely above a whisper. "Playing with clay is calming." I saw her Adam's apple bob up and down as she swallowed. What remained of her once thick, black curly hair was only a few thin wisps. Her skin gave off a greenish hue and was so thin I could almost see the light through the other side.

"The doctor recommends it as my therapy since it is so soothing, honey. He says that when your body is sick like mine is, there is nothing to do but relax. Clay between my fingers helps keep my inner mind at peace, even when my outer body is . . ." her eyes clouded over ". . . falling apart."

I didn't understand what she said—I was too young to understand the life-snuffing horrors of bone cancer—but a wave of sadness swept over me. It started in my stomach and radiated throughout my entire body, meeting and swelling in my jaw. I clenched my aching jaws together, trying to break through the prison of pain. My throat felt dry and fiery, and my body heavy, as if gravity was pushing it deeper and deeper into the floor. I needed to lighten the heaviness, to stop sinking into the floor of sadness. I knew I shouldn't cry and choked back my tears. I forced a smile and said, "We can do therapy together, Auntie Jill!"

The beads of water that had collected along the rims of her eyes spilled down her cheeks. She swept them away with the back of her hand and, with a trembling, choked-up voice, said, "We can, Sophia. We will." As she pressed her ice-cold lips against my forehead, I shivered. And that is the last memory I have of Auntie Jill. ★

A Girl and Her Rock Star
by Stephanie Feldman

You walk home in new blue jeans, skipping such an easy beat, true rhythm, rock and roll across the pavement, reaching with its hands of broken glass for ankles, knees, and thighs that dream of blue-skinned San Francisco Bay. Forgive the blood its panics and its joys; the drums promise lightning, guitars cry out. You're holding in one hand the feeling of his hand, in one hand the newest record, remembering the kiss beside the bus, his silence, his smile. The stereos fly. ★

SEPARATION

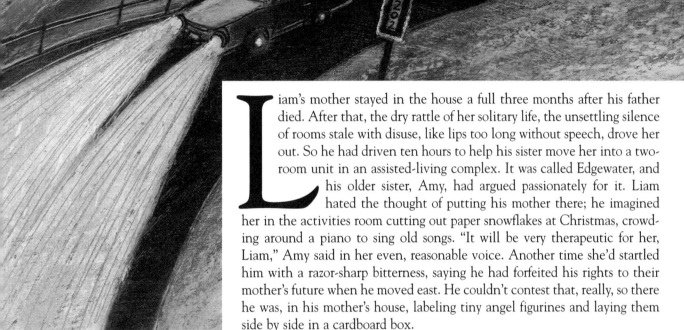

By Sarah Fahey

contemporary
FICTION

Liam's mother stayed in the house a full three months after his father died. After that, the dry rattle of her solitary life, the unsettling silence of rooms stale with disuse, like lips too long without speech, drove her out. So he had driven ten hours to help his sister move her into a two-room unit in an assisted-living complex. It was called Edgewater, and his older sister, Amy, had argued passionately for it. Liam hated the thought of putting his mother there; he imagined her in the activities room cutting out paper snowflakes at Christmas, crowding around a piano to sing old songs. "It will be very therapeutic for her, Liam," Amy said in her even, reasonable voice. Another time she'd startled him with a razor-sharp bitterness, saying he had forfeited his rights to their mother's future when he moved east. He couldn't contest that, really, so there he was, in his mother's house, labeling tiny angel figurines and laying them side by side in a cardboard box.

Yesterday he and Amy had met the program director of Edgewater. "Please, call me Tim," he told them. "I like everyone to feel even here." Liam stared at the severe part in Tim's hair just above the sparse eyebrows that were knitted in a crease of perpetual sympathy. Tim spoke as if in fear of the harsh, abrasive sounds of consonants. He insulated his words with a tiny cushion of air and a slight recoil of his head. Liam noticed the tremor that ran through the slick, shining umbrella tree in the corner of the office when the heat kicked in. He was silent, staring at the serene landscape paintings, the gray carpet, the pale green walls. Amy was nodding and smiling overeagerly and saying yes, wouldn't the grounds be lovely in the spring, and oh, wouldn't their mother love it here with people who share her interests, and of course, a tour would be fantastic. Amy whistled slightly as she spoke to Liam through her tight smile, telling him to come along, he must have questions after all.

Liam pulled books from the shelves in his mother's living room. He was reading parts of them, obscure novels mostly, enjoying his inefficiency. He ran his wide thumb through the dust on the bindings, allowed the books to fall open, cleaving naturally where the unbalanced weight of repeated readings lay like wax over the pages. When Amy came in and saw how little he had accomplished, she cocked her head, birdlike, to one side and made a face that was like biting into something sour. "Come on, Liam, you know this needs to be done by the weekend. Why don't you go upstairs and pack up her room?" He obeyed wordlessly, his sandals scuffing the floor as he passed her. She spun away to the kitchen, long whip of hair lashing first one shoulder, then the other.

He stepped into his mother's bedroom carrying the box from the microwave he had bought her two years ago

Liam hated the thought of his mother living at Edgewater, cutting out paper snowflakes in the activities room, crowding around a piano to sing . . .

for Christmas. He set it down beside her bed and ran his fingers over the thick, velvety bedspread. One by one he pulled out the saint cards wedged in the frame of her mirror, their edges curling and fading to a jaundiced yellow. Saint Anthony, patron saint of lost causes; Saint Theresa of the rose. He wrapped an elastic twice around the pile and set it in the box along with a bunch of plastic flowers, unnaturally bright blues and pinks like cotton candy. Finally, he took the statue of Mary down from the top of a cabinet. He laid it in tissue paper on the bed and stood, unable to wrap it and put it away, as if she might suffocate there in the dark. Ever since Sunday school in second grade, when Mrs. Frasier had taught them the story of Mary, he had hated looking at that statue. He hated the impossible serenity of her modest, demure smile, the arms outstretched in what had always seemed to him more an

indifferent shrug than a forgiving embrace. She was so unlike anyone he had known, so unlike his own mother with her ravenous need for approval, her jealous and protective anger. There was no hunger in the ceramic face, the sightless eyes. None of the despair, no rage over a murdered son. No resentment for what was asked, no knowledge of human death as she ascended, whole-souled, to heaven. He jumped when Amy stepped into the room and he heard her wet, impatient breathing. She rolled her eyes and stepped past him, wrapping the statue and packing it away. She tapped the box with her toe and told him to take it down to the car.

There were already ten boxes in the back of the Nissan, and Liam slid this one in behind. He flinched at the eggshell-thin sound of glass against glass, remembering all the tiny figurines in this box. He climbed in and drove toward Edgewater, past the church, its sharp spire scratching at the clouds.

The Virgin Mary was so unlike his own mother with her ravenous need for approval, her jealous and protective anger . . .

After Liam had dropped off the boxes at his mother's unit, he drove back to the house. He could see Amy through the window, moving quickly from shelves to boxes, arms full of their mother's things. He turned and headed into the backyard where the old chicken coop stood, empty except for his father's old toolshed. The path that led down to it had been nearly washed away in the six months since Liam's father went to the hospital. It was slick with mud, the remnants of a few planks rotting, crumbling under his feet. Inside, he rubbed at his eyes as if the dim half-light were something he could wipe away. The floor was covered under a thin layer of graying sawdust; Liam kicked it up as he stepped over to the workbench. The remnants of unfinished projects were strewn across it, paintbrushes stiffening in a rusty coffee can, grocery store receipts with his father's lists on them: two six-foot two-by-fours, one gallon primer, two-inch dry-wall screws. Liam slipped the scraps of paper into his pocket and tried to begin packing the tools. Three times he began, gathering hammers and drill bits, then putting them down again. He found a bucketful of two-penny nails, warped where his father had pried them out of a piece of wood, and stopped

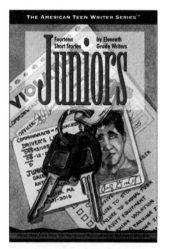

trying to pack. He stood a moment, running his fingers over the benchtop, and then knelt to take a handful of the twisted nails. Dropping them into his pocket with the papers, he stepped back outside. A rusty padlock hung on the doorframe, and with some effort Liam managed to close it. He didn't know where the key was, but he knew Amy would never come back here to ask him about the coop. He left everything there, exactly as it had been, as if someone would be returning shortly to finish some piece of work, momentarily interrupted.

Amy sat at the kitchen table eating ramen noodles, her legs folded under her. "Want some?" he heard her say. He watched her hold up a spoonful until the yellowish strands slithered back into the broth. He shook his head and sat down opposite her. A pair of house finches perched on the bird feeder Liam's father had built years ago. A blue jay left a tree branch with its gasping flight: wings flash, fold in close in surrender to gravity, then flap again to defy it. He and Amy watched the birds with all the desperate intensity of strangers left unexpectedly alone in a room. "Dad's birthday was Saturday, you know," she said. "I drove to the cemetery and sang to him." No words passed between them after that, and Liam waited a long moment before rising to kiss his sister and take his coat. He flipped the radio on as he stopped the Nissan at the end of the street, turned left, and sped toward the highway.

He hadn't meant to drive home tonight, but he knew he couldn't stay in that house. He drove along Route 202, a mountain highway winding, tentative as an apology, around the base of the slopes. The harsh glare of the headlights pooled in the road's dips and hollows; the wind, flecked with leaves and scraps of paper, churned among the pines beside the road. Twice, he saw the gleam of animal eyes over on the shoulder as they caught the light. He could picture Amy, standing awkwardly at their father's grave, singing "Happy Birthday" to the gray tombstone, her song thin in the grayer air. And then, when she was finished, hearing the wind through the cattails along the river. He imagined her staying a moment, until the cold coiled up in her pockets, and she turned to go.

He stopped at the Dunkin' Donuts off Exit 57 and continued toward home, holding the steering wheel in the hollow just under his knee as he wrestled with the plastic cover on his coffee cup. It had just begun to rain and beads of water slid down the windows. He finally settled his coffee into the cup holder to let it cool and reached over to adjust the radio. Vapor rose from the cup and condensed in a small spot on the windshield, steam transubstantiated, trying to join the cold rain outside. ★

The Glue Jar

By Aarti Gupta

Memory can play cruel tricks on the mind. It will have you record some of the most insignificant details and lose the ones that you would do anything to remember.

Like any other day at St. Mary's Convent School, we were all sitting in our neat, straight rows, faithfully doing the task assigned. The boys were in their gray pants and the girls in gray, pleated, knee-length skirts. Everyone was wearing a white, long-sleeved shirt with the school name and symbol embroidered in maroon and gold on the pocket. Tiny feet in black shoes kicked through empty space because of legs too short to reach the floor. The daily pattern was interrupted when a messenger from an older class entered.

"Class, I will return in a few minutes. I want you to continue with the social studies lesson. When you are done gluing the continents down, color in the oceans blue because on a map, blue means water. OK? Monitor One, you are in charge until I return." And with that, Miss Needhi left.

I wonder where she's going. Teachers get to have all the fun. This is too sticky and gooey. Can't we cut out more shapes? Elmer's glue makes a big mess. The brush glue bottle would make this easier.

"I should get one of those glue jars with a brush in it. That would make it so much easier!" I offered this random thought to no one in particular.

"What are you talking about?"

I turned in the direction of the voice. It was the boy behind me. He had short black hair that formed a straight line across his forehead. His skin was wan and pale, a great contrast against his hair.

There's something about him. What is it? Oh, I remember. He's Miss Needhi's nephew. Yes, that's it.

"I said that if I had one of those glue bottles that come with a brush, it wouldn't be so hard to glue these things down. The brush would spread the glue better."

"I'm not deaf! I heard what you said. But what glue bottle with a brush are you talking about? There's no such thing," he stated coolly, as if he had all the knowledge in the world.

"Yes, there is!"

"No, there's not, because I would have seen it if there was one."

"What's all the noise back there? Don't make me come back there!" threatened the monitor with the power he now possessed. Usually he was very quiet and kept to himself. Absolute power corrupts absolutely.

Why do boys always think that they're so smart and important? If they were so smart, they wouldn't act so stupid. Next year when I get the highest grade on the final exam, I'll be the monitor and then I'll show them what a real monitor is supposed to be like!

Silence. Then a few seconds later I said, "I've seen one of those glue jars."

"I bet you haven't!" said Miss Needhi's nephew.

"I bet you I could even get one of those."

"How can you get something that isn't real?"

"I'll bet you anything that I can bring one in tomorrow."

"Fine. The bet's on."

"Fine," I agreed.

We were too young to realize that in order for a bet to work there needs to be a wager.

What was I doing? What was I thinking? Where had I seen that bottle? I knew I'd seen it, but where? Or was that a dream? Maybe I could take a stick and tie some bristles to it and then put it in a jar full of glue.

With these thoughts in my head, I started my walk home. That walk home was, and still is, a blur in my mind. I didn't notice anything on that walk because all that mattered was getting that glue bottle—one way or another. I didn't even notice that I had reached my house until my sister nearly pounced on me, asking if I wanted to play. I was unsuccessful in finding a glue bottle with a brush, and I was unable to tie some bristles onto a stick.

On the way to school the next morning, I again became absorbed in my thoughts, this time trying to think of excuses for my failure.

I know what I'll say. I'll say that the bottle broke on my way to school and that was the only bottle I had.

As I stood in the doorway to the classroom, the excuse no longer seemed valid. It was darker in there than it had ever seemed before. Taking a deep breath, a very deep breath, I entered, preparing for the humiliating defeat ahead. I scanned the room for my adversary.

He's not here. Maybe he got scared because he thought I'd bring one in! I feel so happy. Why is everyone so loud? Where's Miss Needhi and the sister? Shouldn't we be learning something right now?

"Guess what? Guess what?" the girl closest to the door asked me.

"What? What?" I replied, slowly catching the excitement in the room.

"Miss Needhi's nephew is dead! You know, the boy who sat behind you. His little brother scared him when he was at the top of some stairs in their house, and he fell down. They were taking him to the hospital. The road was really bumpy so the car kept bouncing up and down, up and down, and so he died in the car."

That day everyone was let out of school at noon. That was an unprecedented event. Never before, to my knowledge, had the school been closed without a holiday explanation.

Why do boys always think they're so smart and important? If they were so smart, they wouldn't act so stupid.

The babysitter was startled to see me home so soon. After a thorough interrogation about the event, she left me to myself. I was very sorry that Miss Needhi's nephew had died. I knew what death was. I wasn't stupid. It was when someone can never come back. I was six years old. He didn't know he had won; he never would know. Still, I hadn't quite lost, had I? I was sorry and happy at the same time. That was all the thought I

gave to the matter—then.

The next day one of the sisters came to see our class. She was new. I could tell because I had never seen her before. Her white wimple was freshly starched and there were a few strands of black hair—escapees from her tight bun—all around her face. With rosary beads in one hand and the forefinger of the other hand on her lips, she quieted the class.

"Miss Needhi's nephew is dead! You know, the boy who sat behind you. His little brother scared him when he was at the top of some stairs and he fell down."

"As you all know, Miss Needhi's nephew passed away two days ago. She loved him very much. Right now, she's very sad. You all can make cards for her, to make her feel better. Inside them write, *We will miss him dearly. He was a good boy.* Here—I'll write it on the board for you to copy. You can give them to Miss Needhi when she returns tomorrow."

We all set to the task as if it were a math lesson, instead of a showing of sympathy and sorrow.

Miss Needhi was surrounded by twenty-nine children the next day, all eager to offer their tokens of sympathy. I was not one of the twenty-nine. I was standing aside, the last person in line. Unlike the others, I wasn't very eager to give her my card. I hesitated. The pattern broken, she looked at me. Her gaze focused on mine. Her eyes were small, swollen, and red. I didn't know what that meant. All I knew was that there was something wrong.

This doesn't feel right. Maybe I should say something to her. Maybe I should tell her about the glue jar. Should I tell her I didn't really know him?

Then the sister came to stand next to me. She was silently instructing me to give Miss Needhi the card. I quietly surrendered my false sympathy; Miss Needhi, knowing her part in this formality, quietly took it. Like all the other twenty-nine children, I'd written, *We will miss him dearly. He was a good boy,* even though it was a lie. How did I know he was good? I had never spoken to him before. In fact, I did not even know the meaning of "dearly."

In doing as I was told and following everyone else, I have most likely been forgotten by Miss Needhi. Yet, I have not forgotten her. Miss Needhi was never quite the same after that, especially toward our class. She was cold, just as cold as our thirty identical cards must have been to her. However, that is not the only factor contributing to my residual guilt. Over the past ten years I have forgotten his name. Hard as I try, I cannot remember it. Had I ever known it? After ten years, I'm not even sure of that. ★

Miss Dickinson, You and I Would Not Have Been Chums

You're nobody? How very sad—
To live a life so flat
That you must scurry from the world
Like a mouse before a cat.

How lonely to be nobody
Oblivion can't make you free—
How much you missed by taking refuge
In transparency.

I love Earth's glorious expanse
And all its flaws could not
Persuade me to hide in a universe
No bigger than my garden plot.

When I emerge from my cocoon,
I'll be a butterfly
With freedom to sip from every flower
That blooms under Creation's sky.

But you emerged a small plain moth
To waste your precious days
In flitting from your own race,
From its fire's intense gaze.

Or did your chrysalis ever crack
Until the day you died?
Perhaps you spent the rest of your years
A child rapt up inside.

Where was the color in your life
When all you wore was white?
Why were you content to be a moth—
To stare longingly into the light?

Still, Miss Dickinson, though we may be
As different as day and night
We share one essential in our souls—
You and I both live to write.

—Elizabeth Swiney,
Ninth grade, School of St. Mary,
Tulsa, Oklahoma

Dreams From France

Sluggish July twelfth and sifting
through the mess
of her headache,
it was hot so humid hot her last day in France
that the language
dripped off her like sweat,
all the words
she used to know
splattering mispronounced
on the cobblestones of
that ancient city.

Dryly the remnants of July twelfth
pounded through her
gateless window;
one final hour
en français and
he appeared for dinner,
pushed the shadows around on his plate with
the bent tines of a cafeteria fork.

Perhaps it was not just she
who had forgotten how to talk.
There were no words on his plate,
no matter which corner he banished his food to.
The two of them misplaced their vocabulary,
accidentally let it fall
over the windowsill of her room
with the ashes of a crumpled cigarette.
She would say,
"hier soir, hier soir . . ."
and she would say
it can't be over. I need another dance—
I need to stay in France and live in French,
and she would say, if she knew the way
to place her lips and tongue in order to speak,
speak to me,
but useless she could not penetrate the silence,
she found no words and time was passing:
he knew no language and the minutes clacked,
the minutes clicked on
(ne pars pas, ne pars pas)
quietly July
twelfth
dissolved from her.

—Maggie Goodman,
Eleventh grade, Lakeridge High School,
Lake Oswego, Oregon

The East Pole

By Jenny Smith

The power was out when I broke through the heaviness of sleep. There were no harsh red numbers to cut through the darkness of my room. My alarm clock was oddly void of light. I briefly considered going back to sleep, but then thought back to the night before and wondered if the impending snowstorm had hit.

When my dad walked in to wake me, I was standing at my window, pensively watching the wind rearrange snowdrifts on the quiet street. He hadn't knocked.

"Tracy needs a babysitter."

I frowned. "I already have plans for tonight."

"No. Now." It wasn't a question. He stepped out of the room, closing the door behind him. Not certain of what was going on, I pulled on jeans and a sweatshirt and gazed out the window distastefully.

Downstairs, the house was quiet without the constant hum of electricity. The snow was coming down in thick blasts and the walls creaked under the weight. An illuminated whiteness coming from the piles against the sliding glass doors made the kitchen seem foreign and strange. I sat down and pulled on my boots as my mom padded into the room.

"Sorry to wake you," she whispered, in deference to the gentle hush of morning and the silence that accompanied the fallen snow, even though everyone was up. "There was some sort of emergency at church or something. She was desperate."

I nodded and stretched to find the arm of my jacket. We lived down the street from the minister of our church and often watched her two little girls during special events and emergencies. Just not usually so early.

I pulled on a hat and stood beside the door for a moment before finally shoving it open, pushing aside mounds of heavy snow. The street was yet unplowed, though a lone set of brave tire tracks showed that someone had ventured through. The snow came down at a slant, cutting between my scarf and hat as I stepped carefully where the car had driven. I squinted and listened to the wind and the otherwise noiseless street. A sudden chill ran through me, not so much from the cold as from the eerie silence. I hurried on.

Their house was warm and I let myself in, shaking off the wet snow on the mat. I could hear the TV upstairs, and Mark talking on the phone in the kitchen.

"Good morning," I smiled brightly when Tracy came down.

She forced a half smile but looked upset. Mark hung up the phone and grabbed his wife's jacket for her. They began rushing out the door, grim-faced, then suddenly seemed to remember I was there.

Flustered, she pointed upstairs. "The girls have had breakfast and are watching a movie. I have no idea what time we'll be back."

I nodded.

"Do you know the Pierces?" she asked. I shook my head and she went on, "The husband had a heart attack this morning and died. She's pregnant and has four kids. We have to go to the hospital, then go back and tell the kids. So I have no idea when we'll be home. The roads are bad."

I nodded quietly and watched them walk out the door together with a sigh, then headed up the stairs solemnly. The girls were dancing around with cartoons on in the background. They giggled and flung themselves at me when I cracked open the door. I couldn't help imagining four children playing happily, not able to know that in an hour or so, their whole lives would change once the terrible news was delivered. Why is it that life's great burdens always seem to fall

MEMOIR

upon those ill-equipped to handle them? Or perhaps God simply trusts them more to handle what others cannot. I wasn't sure. Either way, it didn't seem fair. I looked past the icy patterns on the window at the snow, my heart wrenching for the family.

"Do you know the Pierces? The husband had a heart attack this morning and died. She's pregnant and has four kids . . . We have to go there and break the news."

"Look outside," cried Sarah, the younger girl. "It's just like the North Pole!"

"Yes, it is," I agreed, pulling her onto my lap.

"And the South Pole!" Emma chimed in.

"That's right," I said, my mind wandering.

"And the East Pole!" Sarah continued.

"There is no East Pole, dummy," Emma told her little sister condescendingly.

I saw tears start to well up and her lower lip tremble. "Yes, there is! Isn't there?" she asked me, her voice pleading.

"Of course there is," I assured her.

"Then why doesn't anybody ever talk about it?" Emma challenged me.

I thought carefully for a moment. "Well, it's kind of a mysterious place."

"Like heaven?"

"Exactly."

"Yeah, but people talk about heaven," she countered.

"Well, the truth is, not a lot of people know about the East Pole."

"Why not?"

I groaned inwardly and my mind raced. "Because it's a place where nobody ever cries or is sad."

They both smiled and I could see them trying to imagine it. "Why wouldn't everyone want to go there then?"

"Well, everyone does," I said, stumbling over my words, "but it's kind of like heaven, where you have to go through a lot of other stuff first."

"Like what?"

I thought furiously. "Let's see. If something very sad happens to you in your life," I told them, thinking of the family that their parents were with at the moment, "then later, you get a chance to go to a place where you'll always be happy. Kind of like a reward for going

through the bad stuff."

"Oh. Like when I get to stay up late if I eat all my carrots?"

"Exactly."

The phone rang and I jumped up gratefully to go answer it, leaving the two girls contemplating the East Pole.

"Hello?"

"Hi, it's Tracy. I just wanted to let you know we're on our way home."

"OK, great."

"And thanks for coming over on such short notice." She sounded tired.

"No problem."

"That was the hardest thing I've ever had to do."

I nodded, unsure of what to say. Part of me wanted to rush forth and tell her how sorry I was and how much my thoughts had been consumed by it since I had heard. But the other voice begged me to remain silent and not pretend to understand such a deep sorrow. For I had never experienced anything like it. She went on without me saying a word.

"I'll be home in fifteen minutes."

"OK, bye."

The house was cold and the windows were covered in icy condensation. I peered out and gazed at the houses across the street. In a house just like those at this very moment, a family is in shock, I thought. Their whole life has changed.

The snow showed no sign of letting up. If anything, it was coming down harder, in great sheets of whiteness. The street outside looked peaceful, settled back and absorbing the inclement weather.

By this time tomorrow the street would be plowed and the sun would reflect brightly off the clean, layered snow. I knew that everything would soon look wonder-

"The truth is, not a lot of people know about the East Pole. It's a place where nobody ever cries or is sad."

ful. Magical, even. The clouds would step aside to let the sun's rays stretch through, and the fresh snow would shimmer beneath them. There would once again be life out on the streets.

But just then, looking out through the whiteness at the rocking trees and swaying branches, it was hard to be certain. ★

Sweaty Palms

By Daniel Becker

contemporary FICTION

O ut of habit, I wiped my moist, clammy hand on my shirt before taking A. J.'s in a halfhearted grip.

"Good luck. Be strong," he said in a voice that could almost pass as serious. He nodded and shook my hand.

A. J. was always doing that; it was his thing, shaking hands and saying something corny. You could just be passing him in the hall or on the street, and he would stop you, give you a shake and a nod, and say something like, "Keep up the good work." It was sort of strange, he and I being best friends: A. J. with his obsession with handshaking, me with my paranoia about grody palms.

I'm not kidding when I say my hands are grody. They are virtual Popsicles; my fingers have rough calluses in weird places, and my palms are always—*always*—sweaty. Whenever I take my hand off a desk at school, I always find a residue of perspiration (which I always wipe away with my sleeve) in the exact shape of the hand. I am fairly notorious for this affliction, too. The entire tenth grade knows not to lend me a calculator, unless they want to find little puddles on all the keys. My hands are so gross that I have contemplated issuing a personal policy of "no palm touching," replacing high-fives and handshakes with "fist bashes" and hugs. This last handshake, though, I did not mind. This time, my hands had an excuse to be sweaty.

I was about to call someone. A girl. To ask her out.

Through typical high-school channels, it had come to my attention that a certain young female had taken an interest in me. Now it was my move. Although I was sixteen years of age, I had no experience with this sort of thing. I was nervous. I was *very* nervous.

"You gonna call or not?" A. J. egged me on.

I did not respond. Instead, I gathered my courage, searched my disheveled room for my phone, picked it up, and dialed seven numbers. The phone rang once, twice. I started to quiver. The third ring. Someone picked up.

"Hello," a sweet, feminine voice answered.

"Uh, hi," I responded quickly. Probably too quickly.

"Is this Jonah?"

"Yeah! Hey, listen. I was just on my way out, but I thought I'd give you a call," I lied, opening a quick escape in case I got shot down. "Some of us—you know, me, A. J., Mike, maybe some others—are going to a movie tomorrow, and I was wondering if you wanted to go."

"Sure."

"All right! We'll pick you up around seven. I really gotta go. See ya tomorrow."

"Yeah, bye!"

I put down the phone, pulled my sleeve over the heel of my hand, and wiped the receiver.

"You da man! You da man!" A. J. yelled excitedly.

He had a right to be happy because, as he saw the whole ordeal, phase one of his latest plan was complete. He had been working on this plan for almost a week, ever since that bittersweet night at the Grab 'n' Go.

I was about to call someone. A girl. Although I was sixteen years of age, I had no experience with this sort of thing. I was very nervous.

"I'm telling you, after tonight my personal life is going to be much better," A. J. said.

I kept my eyes on the road and said, "Yup."

From the second my car pulled into his driveway and he jumped in, that was all he would talk about. How much better his personal life was going to be. That was all he said, but I caught his drift. They say people get really close when they can express all their thoughts and feelings to each other in words. I guess A. J. and I are such good friends because we do not even need words to express our thoughts. From that one sentence, I knew he was going to ask a girl out, and I even had a pretty good idea who it was.

He said those words four or five more times before we pulled into the Grab 'n' Go parking lot. I found a good spot—a "pull-through," one I would not have to back out of when we left—and we went in. The Grab 'n' Go combined the worst elements of fast food and a diner. It had rude waitresses and dirty flatware, but it also had a drive-through.

We saw some of our friends sitting in a booth and headed in that direction. As we came closer, they spotted us and called, "Jonah! Apple Jack!"

We slid into opposite sides of the booth. It was a tight squeeze for me, as I sat next to our "big-boned" friend, Mike Baker. The kid was fat, but he refused to acknowledge the fact. He always tagged along when some of us went to play basketball or soccer, but he always ended up on the sidelines, out of breath, within a matter of minutes. A. J., on the other hand, had room to spread out. He was sitting next to Spencer "Stick Boy" Wilson. We were not that close to the quiet, skinny fellow, and I did not know him well.

"So, A. J., how's the movie coming?" Mike asked through a mouthful of hamburger.

I grinned at the mention of A. J.'s latest scheme, but the man behind the plan just grimaced, like you do when you get unexpectedly squirted by a hose. A. J., secretly, was a huge Tom Cruise fan, and one day he got an idea: he was going to make *Top Gun II*. He told everybody that he was going to write and direct it, that I was helping with the script, and that he even got Tom Cruise to reprise his role as Maverick.

I went along with his plans, just for the ride, but A. J. really expected something to come of his little project. Usually, all he got were laughs, but nothing could keep him down.

"Well, we sort of had some financing problems—" A. J. began, straight-faced and in a calm voice.

I jumped in. "Yeah, and now Tom thinks he's some kind of hotshot producer, so we ran into some scheduling conflicts."

"Sure," Mike said. He took a big slurp from his milkshake.

A. J. and I ordered, then we spent the next hour talking and eating. We were in the middle of reminiscing, specifically about how we'd convinced Allen Pertcher that he'd wet the bed at a fifth-grade sleepover (the plot, conceived by A. J., involved pouring a glass of water on Allen's sleeping form, then actually peeing on his pajamas after he peeled them off in disgust. I provided the urine). When A. J. stood up and started staring at the entrance, I turned around to have a look myself.

I began to cross my arms during the Lord's Prayer, and the people next to me would have to reach across me . . .

A large group of kids from our school had come in and they were looking for a booth big enough to seat their whole party. One of them caught my eye immediately. It was Monika Clausen, my next-door neighbor. Her body was perfect, her mesmerizing eyes the color of sparkling blue ice. And she was one of the nicest girls in the world. I had a bit of a crush on her. In fact, sometimes I would stay up late, writing poems about her in a little, key-locked diary I had from when I was younger.

"Is that her?" I asked A. J.

"Sure is. Wish me luck," he said, and departed, but not before doling out handshakes and nods all the way around the table.

Rubbing my two moist hands together, I watched his progress. The group had found a booth, and A. J. was walking toward it, calm, steady. If he was at all nervous, I could not tell. When he got to their booth, he exchanged a few handshakes and positioned himself in a seat directly across from Monika, facing me. The kids she was with were a little more popular than the people we usually hung out with, but that was not a problem. A. J., as the class clown, existed outside the normal social circles. He said something, and everyone at the booth,

Extinct

I rock my daughter in my arms
back and forth, back and forth
and the squeak of the rocking chair
makes me think of bamboo trees and chimpanzees
in pendulum motion.
One day, I'll show my daughter,
all grown up then,
photos of the creatures she never knew
that had been driven away
and whose voices now are
entombed in silence.
I hum softly to my daughter
and her eyelids flutter
like the orange monarchs
that once danced in the wind.

Now we find their wings
torn and scattered
on every sidewalk
that trails through the vanquished forest.
My little girl's blue eyes pop open
and I think of
azure pools where the
elephants once sipped.
Those pools shriveled
like the elephants' skin
and now are murky puddles,
tears from creatures
who roamed here
and constantly remind us
of the time when we walked
hand in hand.

—Carisa Hendrickson,
Tenth grade, Lincoln High School,
Thief River Falls, Minnesota

including Monika, exploded in laughter. Having gained the acceptance of his booth mates, he engaged Monika in quiet conversation for a few minutes. Then he propped his elbow on the back of the booth, cocked his head and said something. He smiled—he was making his move.

I held my breath and watched as his smile gradually dropped into a frown. He left the booth without even shaking anyone's hand. He walked back to our table and slumped down in front of me.

"So," I said.

"Yeah," he responded, looking into his plate of half-eaten fries.

"She gave you the old 'I think of us as brother and sister'?" I asked.

"No." He did not look up. "If she did I would have given her the old 'You ever heard of incest?' No, it was the 'I kind of like someone else.'"

"Ouch. Did she name any names?"

"Yeah." He looked up. He looked up and *smiled.* "You."

I remember the exact moment I started thinking about Monika in a romantic sense. She had lived next door to me for just about forever, but I did not develop my crush until the spring of my fourteenth year.

That was a time in my life that my friends and I do not talk about, and we talk about everything. Defecation, pornography, politics—you name it. But not this. That was the spring my sister and father died.

It was a car accident. My parents were bringing Lauren, my little sister, home from a piano recital which I refused to attend. It happened just three blocks from our house. A Mack truck—which should not have even been cutting through the residential zone in the first place—ran a stop sign and smashed right into the driver's side of our car. Dad and Lauren died on the scene. My mother was hospitalized.

My aunt and uncle, who live only a couple hours away, drove down, and were constantly at my side for the next couple of weeks. The only times they left me alone were when they went to visit Mom in the hospital. They tried to get me to come, but I refused to get in their car. I would not get in any car for a long time after that.

It was during one of those visits to the hospital, less than a week after the accident, that I heard a knock at my front door. I forced myself out of bed—I was just lying there, not actually sleeping—and down the stairs. I opened the door and found Monika standing there on my porch.

She was beautiful. Her straw-colored hair was pulled back in a bun, which was held together by a tortoiseshell clip. She was wearing a black skirt and a black sweater, and the white collar of her shirt poked up above the pullover. She looked perfect. There was one lock of hair that did not get caught in the bun, and it kept falling in her face. While we were standing there on the porch, it was constantly dropping in front of her gorgeous face, and she kept pulling it back. If it were not for that lock of hair, I would have thought she was an angel, sent to answer the prayer that I had been constantly praying over the past five days. I would have thought she was there to take me away to rejoin my sister and father.

She held out a plate of brownies and said, "I am so sorry."

Brownies. That was just like Monika. She was always baking for people. Whenever she was invited to a party, or whenever some tragic or joyful event occurred in someone's life, she whipped up a batch of cookies or a cake. That day, I sure was glad to see those brownies. I had not eaten since it happened.

I invited her in, and suddenly realized I had gone five days without doing a lot more than not eating. Like changing or bathing. She probably could have smelled me next door. I had not shaved either, but at fourteen, that only resulted in a few thin patches of hair on my chin and cheeks. Monika did not seem to mind, though, so I showed her to the living room.

In the living room, we sat down on the couch. It was a white couch, crisscrossed with green stripes. Every so often, one of the boxes the lines made would be filled in with solid green, creating a checkered pattern. We sat there on the couch, Monika talking and me eating.

I did not really listen to what she said, although I could tell she was making a valiant effort to comfort me. Mostly I just ate, and I thought. About my mom, some, but more about Lauren and Dad. Lauren was three years younger than I, and was the kind of sister who would

I really regret not holding my sister's hand. If I had the chance now, I'd grab hold of her little paw and never let go.

always bug you when you were trying to do your homework. I loved her a lot, though, but I never really showed much affection toward her. Dad, though, he was my friend. Ever since I was very young, we would play computer games together. Adventure games, mostly. And sometimes I would read him stories I had written, stories from my diary, stories I shared with nobody else.

Eventually, I finished the entire plate of brownies, and Monika was still talking. So, still caught up in my own thoughts, I started to pick brownie crumbs off the cushions and drop them behind the couch. Dad hated it when I dropped junk behind the couch, but I did it anyway. I picked the crumbs up, one by one with my sweaty index finger, and sprinkled them onto the floor. After a few minutes, there was just one left. I looked at it. It sat there, in one of the solid green boxes, all alone. All alone. I started to cry.

Monika reached out to hug me. She tried to grab hold of my hands, but I would not let her, conscious of their sweaty clamminess. Shortly, she gave up, and I cried on her shoulder for God knows how long. Ever since, I've felt a sort of bond between us. Apparently, so did she.

It was Saturday morning. The morning of the big day, or, as A. J. called it, D-Day. It was very cold and dry for autumn, and everyone was complaining about chapped lips and dry skin. I kept wishing the weather would dry my palms out.

We were sitting in my room again, A. J. and I, only this time we had the company of five or six others. They were the team A. J. had assembled to help fix Monika and me up. Ever since she shot him down, it had become his one desire in life to see the two of us together. I guess he figured that if he couldn't have her, his best friend should. So Top Gun brought these guys in to help realize his dream. Knowing A. J., he had probably assigned them

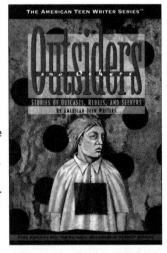

individual roles and even ranks, so that if he was killed in the line of duty, or grounded, they would know what to do and who was in charge.

"We have approximately eight hours to prepare you for the final phase of your mission," A. J. said, sitting in front of me in a director's chair, with his squadron behind him.

"Mission?" I asked.

He ignored me. "You *did* ask her to the movies tonight, but you asked her to come with a group. She probably thinks you are interested in her, but she doesn't know for sure. You have to do something to reassure her tonight."

A. J. turned around to check out his motley party, then stood up and looked at me. "During the movie, you'll have to hold her hand."

"No! Won't do it," I refused, standing up and making for the door.

"And why not?" A. J. countered.

"How many times have we shaken hands, A. J.? You know they're all sweaty and stuff."

"Oh yeah, *muy* bad," he said, and then conferred with his group for a while. He turned back toward me and said, "OK, let's see if we can fix your little problem."

They started asking me questions about my hands— I assumed in hopes of discovering a cure. I could not answer most of their questions, but one I could answer pertained to when I first noticed the problem.

It was about four years before, in church. At the church I went to, we would all join hands to say the Lord's Prayer. Families would hold hands, and then people would scoot through the pews and even across the aisles between pews to form an unbroken chain. It was sort of like a Hands Across America. The whole thing

"You say I'm taking a big risk by not holding her hand; I say if I touch her, my chances with her are nil. Zero. Zilch!"

seemed very reasonable to me—until I hit puberty. Then, at about age ten (I was an early bloomer), holding hands, like many things adults did, seemed absolutely stupid. So I refused to do it.

For about two years I would cross my arms during the Lord's Prayer, and the people standing next to me would have to reach across to continue the chain. Every Sunday, for those two years, Lauren would tug on my shirt and say, "Jonah, why won't you hold hands?"

Finally, when I was about twelve and had outgrown the phase, I gave in. She grasped my hand tightly. Almost immediately, however, she dropped my hand and said, "Ew! It's all cold and grody. Jonah, you got sweaty palms."

At the time, I did not mind—much. It was just an excuse to go on not holding hands. But, looking back, I really regret not holding her hand. If I had the chance now, I would grab hold of her little paw and never let go.

It was six-thirty and M-Hour was rapidly approaching. A. J. and his cronies had been scrabbling around town for the past few hours, looking for a quick way to remedy sweaty palms. Again the ragtag crew had gathered in my room, this time armed with what each individual believed to be the best way to handle my problem.

"OK, Jimmy, you're first," A. J. said.

"Just hold on to these for a while," he said, thrusting out two small cardboard boxes.

"What?" I said.

"Well," Jimmy started to explain, "my brother used to work in a toy store where he was always handling boxes and stuff. You know, when he was straightening the shelves and stuff. Well, he was always complaining that his hands were all dried out, so I thought these might help."

At the time, I was feeling so insecure about my hands that I reached out and took the boxes.

"Tim, you're next," A. J. directed.

A short, awkward-looking kid stepped forward, carrying a black backpack. I knew this guy, and was almost glad to see him in A. J.'s company. Tim was always talking about going hunting or fishing with his "pa," and was always walking up to girls and telling them they were "pertty." Of course, this meant the other kids made fun of him constantly, until A. J. sort of took him under his wing. Since then, he has been known to join in on some of A. J.'s schemes from time to time.

I smiled at Tim, and he smiled back.

He then reached inside his pack, and pulled out a bottle of hand lotion.

"See, I figure your hands are sweating to moisten themselves up, see, and I figure this lotion will stop that on account of it being a moisturizer and all."

Someone at the back of the room called out, "Uh, negative! I talked to this girl who used to have really sweaty palms, too, and she said hand lotion just made it worse."

"Good call, Warren," A. J. put in. "Besides, you don't want to be smelling like hand lotion on a date. But it was a good thought, Tim," he added charitably.

"Anyone else got an idea?"

Silence.

"OK, Jonah, I got one," A. J. continued. He pulled two wads of tissue from his pockets. "Just keep these inside your pockets, and when you feel your hands getting moist, just give 'em a squeeze. I saw it on 'Home Improvement.'"

Instead of taking the tissues, I threw the boxes I was

I looked over at Monika and saw her hand, positioned—maybe purposefully—on her knee, within easy reach. I hesitated.

holding down at A. J.'s feet. "A. J., I'm *not* gonna hold her hand. My hands are disgusting! You say I'm taking a big risk by not holding her hand; *I* say if I touch her, my chances with her are nil. Zero. Zilch!"

I stood up and looked A. J. in the eyes. "Besides, this is just one of your stupid plans, so it could never pan out. It'll be just like trying to get on 'America's Funniest Home Videos.' Just like your movie. Just like trying to set yourself up with her."

For a second, A. J. just stared at me. For just a second. Then he shrugged and called out, "OK, everybody, we gotta move. It's almost seven. Everybody head over to

Jimmy's house. I'll call around eight to give you a progress report. Now let's move!"

At precisely seven, we picked up Monika, and Mike, who was looking as clueless as ever. I cannot tell you how nervous I was, so I relied on A. J. to carry most of the conversation. That was acceptable anyway—I needed to concentrate on my driving.

It was a brisk evening, so we all hurried to get inside the theater. My friend Josh was at his station, tearing tickets. Apparently, he saw us too, as he waved us over.

"What's up, guys?" he asked, showing off a set of popcorn-particled teeth.

"Not much," I answered. "Think you can let us in for free?"

"No prob," he said, waving us through. His managers never seemed to notice, so he almost always let us in.

"Hey, you guys should go see that new one Robin Williams is in," Josh recommended as we walked by.

Josh knew his movies, so we took his advice and headed into Auditorium Three. We found four seats in the back, and Mike and A. J. made sure I sat next to Monika. After a few minutes, the lights dimmed and the previews started. I looked over at Monika and saw her hand, positioned—maybe purposefully—on her knee, within easy reach.

I hesitated. I hesitated for a while, actually. The previews ended and the feature began, but all I could think about was my putrid, festering, sweaty palms. I thought about how revolting some people (A. J. notwithstanding) thought it was to shake my hand, much less hold it. Finally, about halfway through the movie, I thought about Lauren. About how I would never get another chance to hold her hand in church.

I got brave. I reached out my arm and went for the gold. For a second my hand hovered over hers. This was just one of A. J.'s schemes, wasn't it? But if it really was, it would go awry no matter what I did. I made up my mind. I took her hand—her SWEATY, CLAMMY HAND!

I felt angry at myself for a moment, or maybe I felt more like laughing. But then this warm, giddy feeling spread out all over me, starting from my stomach, and I did not feel like laughing anymore. I felt like singing. Like dancing. I looked down at our two sweaty palms, clasped together, and I realized that I was falling in love. ★

DREW, WARRIOR PRINCESS

By Keleigh Friedrich

I was sitting up in bed, a white hotel towel draped across my body, when my mother told me she was pregnant. We had just flown into California from England, where my mom's boyfriend owned a "château."

"It's time for me to move on," she said. "I need my life to begin."

I wanted to ask her where that left me, but I was fifteen and hadn't quite found my voice yet. Instead, I gathered my wet hair into a pile on top of my head and knotted it into a bun. The room suddenly felt very cold.

"Christie Brinkley had a baby after forty, right?" I said in a surprisingly cheerful voice, walking to the window. We were at the Doubletree Hotel in Monterey, in a room my mom's boyfriend was probably paying for. I pulled my towel tight around me and looked out at the black ocean as my mother talked about due dates, gender predictions, baby names. I couldn't think of anything to say.

"You're jet-lagged," Mom said finally. She removed her eyeglasses and lay back in the double bed next to mine. "We can talk in the morning, sweetie. Try and get some sleep."

I couldn't sleep, though. I climbed into bed in just my towel and lay shivering, naked, beneath the covers. My curls unraveled and came spilling across my face and down my back. I thought about calling my father, telling him everything, about Mom dragging me to England to meet Burt, the married businessman with three kids, and about the time she'd taken off for Florida and left me home alone for two weeks. But it was my dad who had left originally; he was the one who had fallen in love with someone else, a hippie to complement his strait-laced conservatism, a woman who wore ponchos and baked bread and painted landscapes in fifty shades of the same color. It was my mom and me who were left behind, who had to sleep in a tent on the beach for eleven days after we were evicted from our house. If it weren't for him, I would be back home in Santa Barbara with my surfboard and my old friends and all the serene normalcy I used to take for granted.

I didn't know what time it was when I woke up. I'd had a dream that I was very old and there was a baby lying in gobs of sticky pink bubblegum on the floor. It was wailing and pawing its little fists at the air, but I wouldn't pick it up.

The muted television was throwing shadows across the walls, casting an eerie glow over my mother's face. She looked like a blank canvas without her usual mask of makeup.

"Are you awake?" I asked.

"Yeah, I guess I'm jet-lagged too." She un-muted the television, and ten minutes later a special report came up about an auto accident involving Princess Diana in Paris.

"Oh, Drew," Mom gasped. She looked over at me. "Did you hear that, Drew? Princess Diana."

I thought about calling Dad, telling him everything, about Mom dragging me to England to meet Burt, the married businessman with three kids . . .

We watched the news until her death was confirmed, and then Mom switched off the television. "This is so crazy," she said. "I wonder if Burt knows."

We drove to a 7-Eleven later in the morning to pick up blueberry muffins, and on the way home Mom told me about how my father had taken her camping for their honeymoon instead of to Europe like she wanted. "He always had to have his way," she sniffed. "He took advantage of the fact that I was sweet, agreeable. I was young, Drew. For God's sake, don't get married young. It ruins you."

I remember pouring my dad's beer for him when I was little. I used to sip the foam before I brought it to him in the living room and climb into his lap as he took his first sip. He wore business suits with too-short ties and Mr. Magoo eyeglasses. My mom would whine to him about his scratchy beard, our small house, her lacking wardrobe. She dressed me up like a fairy princess every Halloween until I was nine, even when I cried and told her I wanted to be a baseball player. Baseball was Dad's favorite sport.

"This baby is going to be so loved," Mom told me as we ate our muffins up in the hotel room. "Burt is a great father. After we lost Adam, your father didn't want to even try again, Drew. So that was it. No more kids. But I've always wanted more kids. I've *needed* more kids."

I wanted to ask when Burt is planning on leaving his wife of eighteen years, but I bit my tongue. My parents had a baby boy five years after I was born, a baby who arrived with the umbilical cord wrapped around his neck. My mother went on antidepressants and kept a picture of his blue little body in her wallet for six years.

"Can't you picture it, Drew?" Mom went on.

"Christmas in England, vacations in Hawaii and the Bahamas. Wait till you see Burt's place in Laguna Beach, sweetie. It's *gorgeous*. It's like a freaking *palace*. Just wait."

That day everyone was talking about Princess Diana. We went to see a friend of Mom's in Pebble Beach, a guy named Matt who looked about twenty-five years old. He told me he was an "entrepreneur." I figured that meant he had a rich daddy.

My mom has a knack for acquiring wealthy friends. After my parents divorced she started going to art galleries and showing up at public auctions just to rub elbows with the financially privileged. She'd wear something low-cut and get asked out every time.

"Your mom's a fine lady," Matt told me over dinner. He raised his champagne glass in her direction. "The first time I met her I thought she looked like an angel. In fact, you look a lot like her, Drew. The same big eyes and dark hair. You guys could be sisters."

I shook my head and smiled sweetly. "No, I resemble my dad," I told him. "He's Belgian."

"Like the waffle?" Matt grinned at me.

I couldn't even bring myself to smile. I looked at my mother. She was sipping a glass of burgundy-colored wine. "Mom," I hissed, "you can't drink that. You're *pregnant.*"

Her cheeks suddenly flushed, and she turned on me

Smoke

Shadows
over puddles of moonlight
across the grass
on cool water.
We float in the current,
running shoes
side by side
on the shore.
Shorts
wet and heavy
cling to sore thighs.

He is fingertips away,
a fire I'm afraid to touch.
Like smoke,
traces of him
in my hair, in my clothes.

—Rachae Probst,
*Twelfth grade, Mead High School,
Spokane, Washington*

with a crimson look. Her jaw hardened into a firm line. "Drew Elizabeth," she growled.

Matt's eyes were darting back and forth between us, a dumb smile still glued to his face. "Lynn?" he squeaked, his hand going to cover hers. She stood abruptly, knocking over her wineglass in the process, and walked out of the room.

I sat very still in my chair. I was vaguely aware of Matt leaving the table to follow her, then voices in the living room, and then the front door opening and slamming shut. I wondered if Mom was going to take off, leave me here in a strange man's condo with nothing but my toothbrush in my pocket and the silver necklace I always wore beneath my shirt, the one my father gave me when I was eight. It looked pretty chintzy, but I liked the feel of the cool chain against my chest.

I pressed my palms against the white tablecloth and took a deep breath. I said today's date in my head: August thirty-first. "Where will we be in the fall?" I had asked Mom in England when I started not being able to sleep at night. "Drew, sweetie, it's summer, it's vacation time, fun time, no-worries time. Don't stress so much. You're just like your father."

I don't remember my father ever stressing, except maybe about money. Yes, definitely about money. I remember finding a bundle of receipts in my mom's purse the year they divorced—hundreds of dollars in Chanel makeup, designer clothes, sexy new shoes. But is that enough reason to leave somebody? Just because they like nice things?

Pretend you're somewhere else, I thought. Don't worry about school or having a place to live. Just close your eyes and imagine the waves in Santa Barbara; see

It was Mom and me who were left behind, who had to sleep in a tent on the beach for eleven days after we were evicted from our house.

yourself paddling out on your surfboard with the salt in your nose and your hair.

I first learned to surf the winter my parents separated. That was the year I started junior high, and every seventh-grader was assigned a ninth-grade "buddy." I was assigned this beautiful blonde goddess named Candace who had legs like a Barbie doll. My best friend at the

time, Wendy Engstrom, was extremely jealous. She'd been hooked up with Theresa Alvarez, who belted out opera tunes in P.E. and wore stretch pants with high heels.

I was in awe of Candace. She played soccer and volleyball and ran track, and one Saturday morning she ran into me at the mall and invited me along with her and her friends to go surfing. It was early December and my

Mom dressed me up like a fairy princess every Halloween until I was nine, even when I cried and told her I wanted to be a baseball player.

parents were in the process of falling out of love. At night I used to lie awake in my bed listening to them, trying to make out every biting, muffled word from their bedroom, while every prolonged silence brought to mind images of them kissing and making up—for good this time. I would hold my breath, praying for the silence to continue through the night, but if I waited long enough the biting, muffled words always started up again.

I borrowed Candace's little sister's surfboard and wore this pathetic purple one-piece bathing suit. It was hideous, and I had no boobs to fill it out. But we went to Ledbetter, the point at the far end of West Beach, because Candace said the slow waves were good for beginners. Her friend Chris, who was a sophomore in high school and had the most underarm hair I've ever seen on a person up close, took me out into the water and showed me how to position myself on my board so that the nose was just barely out of the water. I imagined that underneath the ocean's surface there were little water nymphs who were going to help me get up on my board and not make a fool of myself in front of the goddess Candace and her tan, pot-smoking friends. The first couple of times I just rode in on my stomach back to shore, getting the feel of the waves, but by the end of the day I could stand up long enough to forget about how ugly my bathing suit was. It was wonderful.

I went with the Surf Sluts, as Candace and her friends called themselves, almost every weekend after that. We sometimes went to Graveyard, just south of East Beach, where the Santa Barbara Cemetery sits atop the cliffs and, as these cliffs erode, slowly slides its tombstones and corpses down to the sand. We didn't surf at

Graveyard, though; we just passed around joints and mumbled a lot, and this was the first time I ever had anything to do with drugs. Even as I was inhaling, I was picturing my fifth-grade D.A.R.E. officer who had the most beautiful blue eyes and blond hair. He used to set out an "anonymous question box" for kids to ask him about

"This baby will be so loved! Burt's a great father!" I wanted to ask her when Burt is planning on leaving his wife of eighteen years.

drugs, and my friends and I would put notes in saying, "Are you married?" and "Do you know how cute you are?"

The day my dad left for good, in early March, when I came home from school and found him on the front stoop with a suitcase, trying frantically to lock the door behind him, I went to Devereaux Point. This is where tar seeps into the ocean from dozens of underwater vents, and sometimes even the beach is covered with it. Mom and Dad had given me a board for Christmas, so I got a ride from one of the male Surf Sluts, Chris with the hairy armpits, and we sat in the tarry sand during twilight. Chris thought I was acting hyper. He offered me some pot to mellow me out, but I started crying and said, "It's OK that there's tar, right? I mean, it's natural, right?"

And I went flying off with my board into the water, panting and sputtering with each swell, and when I came out I had tar in my hair and on my board, and everywhere.

"The wind is blowing onshore," Chris said. "That's the worst, Drew. Why are you so weird? Tar sucks, doesn't it?"

I didn't talk all the way home that night. My father had been shaking when he finally got the key in and heard me behind him. "I love you, Drew," he'd said, but his eyes were swimming and darting around, and when I went inside there was nothing of him remaining.

Laguna Beach was the perfect surfing town. I tried, at first, to be a Laguna Babe. I started school two weeks late, after Mom and I moved into a tiny apartment a couple miles from Burt's "palace," and I resolved to be happy there. I walked into my first-period class wearing baby-blue thongs and little board shorts and even a Dragon sweatshirt, one of the hard-core boarding brands that was right up there with Volcom. Two cute guys stopped me after school and asked if I surfed, and when I told them I did they invited me along with them to catch some waves at Salt Creek. But when I ran all the way home to grab my board, I found it lying in the middle of the living room floor next to my mother, in a pile with Mom's wedding ring and our old sewing machine and about a dozen other things.

"Whatcha doin' home, Drew?" Mom asked distractedly.

I walked hesitantly into the room and stood over my board, facing her. "What are you doing?" I said, my voice quivering only slightly.

She blew some loose strands of dark hair out of her eyes and looked away from me, busying her hands with a stack of overdue bills. "Drew, sweetie, I can't depend on Burt forever. The collectors have been calling—"

"Yeah, Mom, I know. I lie to them just about every day."

"Yeah, well, sweetie, I'm sorry it has to be that way, but I don't make the rules. And now we're in a little bit of debt and Burt's away on vacation for a while, and until I can find a job we really need to sacrifice some of these . . . these superfluous things just lying around the house . . ."

I felt my heart deflate and speed up at the same time. I looked from her face to my precious board, and back again. "My *surfboard?*" I squeaked.

Mom cleared her throat. "Well, sweetie, I'm making sacrifices too, and it's not permanent or anything. We'll be able to get you another one pretty soon, you know? It's just for now. It's just one of those things we have to do. OK? OK, sweetie?"

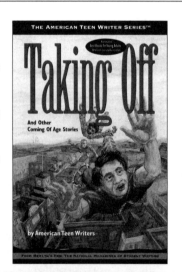

I watched her for a moment or two. I knew I wouldn't be getting another board anytime soon. Her hands shook as she shuffled the stack of bills, pretending to glance at each one as she mixed them up like a deck of cards. She was the High and Mighty Queen of Hearts, the cruel and heartless queen who could break me with a weak puff of her breath whenever she wanted. And there was Burt, the court jester juggling two women, and Dad, the one-eyed Jack too wimpy to look anyone full in the face.

Mom lost the baby in October. I still couldn't afford a board, so after school I'd go watch the popular surfer kids in the water, pretending to read a book so I didn't have to meet anyone's eye. The kids at school were all tan, blond, cookie-cutter examples of perfection. They got drunk on the weekends and hung out at an all-age club called Liquid. I went there once with my pretend-friend Lisa and spent the whole night hiding in the bathroom.

"Do you think God is punishing me, sweetie?" Mom asked as I brought her juice and toast. She was curled up in a tight ball in bed, hugging a pillow to her chest. She had been in this position since the day she got home from the doctor's office.

I moved to open the blinds, but she snapped at me. "Leave them," she said. "Why would I want daylight in? Do you think it'll make things better? For God's sake, Drew, grow up. My baby's dead. Another one. I'm the dead-baby woman. The cursed dead-baby woman."

I had washed my mother's bedsheets the day it happened, bleached them until only a pale outline remained of the bloody mess that was her child. I drove her to the doctor, even though I didn't even have my permit yet, because Burt was home with his wife. His wife was an alcoholic. Burt said that once she was in rehab and had her life together, he would talk to her about divorce, but until then, "it's just too complicated." I heard this while I was eavesdropping on one of my mother's phone conversations with him. "I need you, Burt," Mom sobbed. "I need to be with you."

Everything that remained of Mom's baby passed through her until she was "cleaned out," as the doctor had called it. She had cramps and mumbled about Princess Diana in her sleep. On the third night after the miscarriage, she came and knelt by my bed at three in the morning, shaking me until my eyes popped open. There were bags under her eyes.

"Drew, sweetie, come sleep with me," she said. I followed her into her room, climbed into bed next to her. She wrapped her arms around me and rested her cheek against my chest. "My body kills babies," she said. "Do you think I'll get pregnant again, Drew?"

I struggled to keep my eyes open. "Sure," I mumbled. "You'll be happy, Mom. I know you will."

"Happy? Oh, really?" She chuckled. "I need Prozac, sweetie. If your father would send us more money, I could get Prozac. I could be better, sweetie. Maybe you should talk to him. He'll listen to you."

I felt a tear sliding down my chin. "Don't worry, Mom," I said. "I'll talk to him. It'll be OK."

Mom rubbed her cheek against my shoulder. "I love you so much, sweetie," she said. "You're just like me when I was your age. Don't leave me, Drew. Just stay here and we'll be two and two, cozy like peas, two feet in the same sock. We're just alike, baby-love. We're like best

I went flying off with my board into the water, panting and sputtering with each swell, and when I came out I had tar in my hair, on my board, and everywhere.

friends. Just don't leave me, OK? It'd be like chopping off one of my arms."

That was the last thing I heard before I paddled off on my pretend surfboard to dreamland.

"Don't let your mother manipulate you, Drew," Dad told me on the phone. "I believe that she's ill and that she needs help, but she does know how to distinguish between fiction and reality."

"So you're not sending any money?" I said sharply.

I heard him sigh. "Drew, are you all right there? I know things have been rough the last couple months, but how are things normally? Does your mother take care of you?"

I bit my lip, hard. "I'm fine," I said. "So what about the money?"

There was a pause. "I'll send some," he said finally. "But next time, please tell your mother to call me herself regarding money matters. It's not your responsibility, Drew."

"You *made* it my responsibility, Dad," I snapped, and hung up the phone.

For my sixteenth birthday, Mom and Burt bought me

a surfboard. A pink one.

"Burt picked it out himself," Mom said proudly, a smile pulling on her sad blue eyes.

"I thought pink would go nicely with your dark hair," Burt told me. I wanted to tell him to take the surfboard and shove it, but a God-awful pink board was still better than no board at all.

"Thank you," I said, crinkling my eyes to attempt some sort of a smile. "Great choice."

Mom and Burt left that day for a cabin in Lake Arrowhead. "I wish I could take you out to dinner or something, sweetie," Mom said, "but we really need to leave this afternoon. You know, before all the tourists start heading up."

It was the first official day of summer. My sixteenth birthday. Mom had left a card on the kitchen table that morning, unsealed, with *Sweetie-Baby* scrawled in messy handwriting across the front. The card was a teddy bear holding balloons. WISHING YOU ALL THAT YOUR HEART DESIRES ON YOUR BIRTHDAY. Below the message she'd

"I love you, Drew," Dad had said. But his eyes were swimming and darting around, and when I went inside the house, there was nothing of him remaining.

written, *Oh, Drew, you're the best, you know that. I believe in you and you have grown up to be such a beautiful and smart young woman. You can accomplish anything and I love you more than anything. Love Mom.*

"If your father doesn't call, I am going to be so pissed off," she said as she threw some sunscreen into her purse. "Make sure to tell me if he doesn't call, Drew. Oh, and if he does call, try not to mention I'm leaving for a few days, all right? The last thing we need is him breathing down our necks and getting all overprotective, right? I mean, you're sixteen now, for God's sake. You don't need coddling anymore, right? You're practically a woman."

I felt Burt's eyes scan over me at that moment, and I crossed my arms over my chest. "Fine, Mom," I said. "So go. Have a great time."

I went out on my new surfboard that day. I wore an old one-piece and coiled my hair into two Princess Leia buns. That's what I am, I thought. A warrior princess.

After a few uneventful sets, I paddled back in to shore and sat in the sand by some rocks. I waxed down my board as I watched the waves, averting my eyes from

other beach-goers and pretending I was invisible. I leaned my head back against a boulder and envisioned staying out here all day, sleeping by the rocks at night, no one bothering me or acknowledging that I was here.

When I opened my eyes there was a guy staring at me. He was about waist-deep in the water, and when he saw me looking he started walking in toward me. When he got close enough he yelled out, "Hey!"

Another beach-bum psycho. He had bleached blond hair and strong brown shoulders. A man's body.

I didn't say anything until he was almost directly in front of me. Then I looked him full in the face, right into his startlingly green eyes, and said, "Hi."

He said his name was Logan. He smelled like salt water and beer and something else, something sweet like flowers or sugar. His hair was crazy-curled and he pointed to my board and said, "Can I guess your favorite color?"

We talked all day. I told him it was my birthday, and he went and fished some seaweed out of the ocean to make me a crown. When I told him I was sixteen he raised his eyebrows. "I thought you were older," he said.

We stayed at the beach until sunset and then he drove me home. "I like you," he said at my doorstep. I didn't want to go inside and listen to the emptiness. I closed my eyes and thought of the water nymphs that used to help me surf. I wanted to evaporate.

"Where are your parents?" he whispered.

"They flew away," I said, looking over his shoulder to the street.

He grinned mischievously. "Do you have any beer?"

I shook my head. "Wine, maybe. But I don't drink."

He leaned his face in close to me. "But *I* do," he said, grinning like the Cheshire Cat or Jack Nicholson or someone equally terrifying. His face lit up. "Wait a second!" He ran to his van and brought back two beers. "Thank God for coolers," he said. "You want one?"

"A cooler?"

"No, a beer."

"No, I told you. I don't drink."

"Oh . . . well, do you mind if I do?"

I shook my head. I just wanted to bury my face in his T-shirt and breathe him entirely in. "Can we just sit here, on the step?" I said. "Just for a while?"

Logan nodded and sat down next to me. "You sure you don't want to go inside?" he asked.

I raised my eyebrows. "What, so you can have your way with me?" But I didn't want him to leave. There was a lump rising in my throat, and all I could think of was going to sleep tonight with a guy in my head. Finally.

Logan told me he was twenty-four. He was living out of his van right now, working construction. He sang and played guitar in coffeehouses sometimes. He wanted to be like Dan Bern, the folk singer. He also wanted to surf in Australia.

"Have you been in love?" I asked him. The night was starting to blanket us.

He rolled his can of beer between his palms. "Yeah, once, when I was seventeen. Her name was Amber."

I pictured a lithe, honey-haired girl in a sundress. I watched Logan's lips as he talked, his voice filling me. I interrupted him by closing my mouth over his.

He smiled at me as we pulled away. "What are we gonna do, Drew?" he said quietly.

I smiled back. "I don't know, Logan. Are we in trouble?"

He kissed me again, then smirked as his hand skimmed my leg. "We just might be."

I wanted to ask him how many beers he'd had today, but that was too uptight-girlfriendish. "You'd better go," I said.

"You want me to leave?"

"For now, yes."

"Can I see you again?"

"Will you be at the beach tomorrow?"

He smiled. "If you're gonna be there, I will."

I smiled back. "Then I'll see you." He gave me one last kiss and left.

My dad had left a message on the machine. "Hey, kiddo, it's your dad . . . Just wanted to wish you a happy birthday. I was hoping you could come stay with me for a week or two. We could go to Magic Mountain and Raging Waters—all that fun stuff. Anyway, I hope you're having a great day. You should be getting my gift any day now. I love you."

She was the High and Mighty Queen of Hearts, the cruel and heartless queen who could break me with a weak puff of her breath whenever she wanted.

I erased the message and went straight to my room. Here's what I really need, I thought: Logan. To hell with my parents. This is Drew being sixteen.

I saw Logan every day the week Mom was gone.

When I talked to Dad I told him I'd been spending a lot of time with my friend Lisa, and maybe later in the summer I would go visit him in Santa Barbara. Maybe.

"Susan's dying to see you again," Dad said on the third day Mom was gone. Susan was the hippie with the ponchos. He was still with her after all this time. That pissed my mom off. Once, she got drunk and stayed up all night watching movies with me, during which she trashed Susan at every possible interval: "slut" and

"I need Prozac, sweetie. If your father would send us more money I could get Prozac. I could be better, sweetie . . ."

"deflowered flower child" were her favorite labels for the woman she called a "home-wrecker living in sin." That was before she started gold digging and sleeping with any male on two legs.

"Well, tell her I say hi," I replied. When I hung up I went straight for The Rocks. That's what Logan and I called our secluded meeting place. He was already there waiting, a six-pack of beer and a honeydew melon beside him. Logan seemed to love honeydew melon.

"Do you ever worry you'll end up an alcoholic like your father?" I asked him.

He stared out at the ocean. "All the time," he said. "But I figure, hey, whatever's gonna happen . . . it's gonna happen, you know? There's not much I can do about it, you know?"

I stared at him. I saw the honeydew melon juice running down his chin. I saw the plastic bag of marijuana sitting in the sand next to him. I looked down at his huge hands and said his age in my head. When I was six, he was losing his virginity. When I was ten, he was graduating from high school. When I was sixteen . . .

"That's the dumbest thing I've ever heard," I said.

He looked at me, his green eyes startled. "Are we getting feisty now, Drew?" he said with a tiny smile.

I felt sick to my stomach. I wanted to cry.

"What's wrong?" he asked, taking a swig of beer.

I sat quiet as a meadow, my spirit folded neatly in my lap. It had tiny, frail butterfly wings that looked ready to fly away.

"Are you PMS'ing or something?" Logan laughed, touching my arm with his huge hand. I dug my fingers into the cool sand. Twilight was beginning to curtain us like lavender gauze.

"I'm fine," I mumbled. I got a flash of my mother, all shiny and pretty with her lips pursed out like Brigitte Bardot. She always made sure to lean forward a little when she was wearing a bikini, to give her admirers the full view of her assets. She smiled a lot and ran her fingers through her hair.

"We'll be two and two, cozy like peas, two feet in the same sock. We're just alike, baby-love. We're like best friends. Just don't leave me, OK?"

I frowned. Would you rather be completely friendless and leaking loneliness out of your soul, or have one person who may not necessarily meet the criteria for your ideal mate, but who's there and wanting you, and the sun is setting like rainbow sherbet melting all over the kitchen counter?

"You smell good," I said. I looked him full in the face. "You always smell good. And one time I went to this nude beach in Santa Barbara called More Mesa. I went with the Surf Sluts—"

"What?"

"—and they all stripped down, but I was only thirteen and had just gotten my first training bra the day before."

Logan stared at me for a long, long moment. His lips twitched into a smile. He set down his beer. He spread his fingers over my bare stomach and laughed when I flinched at the shock of his cold hand against my skin. I thought of my mother and me each putting one foot into the same sock. She would look at me and giggle like a schoolgirl, and she'd brush my hair from my face and say, "See, you're just like me, sweetie. We're two and two."

And then he was touching me and kissing me, and it all melted together with the ocean and the sand like a summer dream.

By Day Eight I started worrying that Mom wasn't coming home. She had called once from Lake Arrowhead and left a message, but Dad's calls were becoming more frequent and suspicious. He'd ask to talk to Mom and I'd say she was at the store or in the bathroom. We hardly had any food left in the refrigerator, which didn't really matter anyway since I'd stopped eating once I met Logan. Something about him tied my stomach in knots twenty-four hours a day. It was like my time was finally here. Maybe my life had begun.

Every night Logan asked me to spend the night in his van or let him in my house.

"You don't trust me?" he asked.

I shook my head. "We're crazy, Logan. We're totally psychotic."

"Ahh, geez, Drew. What the hell is this? Why are you doing this?"

"Doing what?"

That night he came and threw rocks at my bedroom window. I woke up scared and didn't even look in the mirror before creeping to the window.

"Hey," he whisper-yelled. "Can you come out?"

He thought my mom was home by now. I'd never bothered to tell him that she was prolonging her trip.

I went outside in my funky striped socks, my silk boxers, and threadbare tank top. I wasn't wearing any underwear.

"You're crazy," I said. "What are you doing?"

I felt his eyes taking me in. Haha, I thought. Sexpot at sixteen.

"I wanted to see you," he said. There was something daring in his eyes. He leaned against his car and pulled me toward him, his hands drifting over me. "You're so hot," he whispered, his lips cool against my neck. I tasted beer on his breath and ran my fingers through his hair. He felt so good that tears somehow came to my eyes.

"I love you," he said.

I stopped. I pulled away. "What the hell are you saying?"

The Composer

Her shadow floods the light wood floor,
spreads black over planks and nails by the rocker.
Distressed and thin, she sits in her apron.
Her hair tied at the nape of her neck
binds the great length of gray into a bun.
Her shoes tap the floor on every rock of the chair.
She sings, snapping peas into her big brown bowl.
Like a cobbler's, her hands move fast
and the peas shoot from their long pods.
The plop of the peas, the rattle of the bowl,
     the cracking of their skin.
She thinks to herself, it might rain, and leaves her
     station on the porch.
The kitchen will suit just fine.

—Gwyn Lederman,
Tenth grade, Westfield High School,
Westfield, New Jersey

"What, I can't tell you I love you?"

"Don't screw with me, Logan. I'm not like the other girls. I'm not going to believe something just because it sounds good or it flatters me."

He was trying to kiss me again and I gave up. He was drunk.

"You shouldn't have driven," I said. "You're gonna kill yourself." I took him by the hand and led him up the stairs to our apartment, then into my room.

"But your mom—"

"No, she's out. Don't worry." I helped him take off his shoes. I snuggled under the covers with him and rested my head against his chest. He felt strong and warm, like a man.

I hardly slept at all, but it was the nice kind of awake that feels like you're sharing a secret with the world, not insomnia like I'd been having the past couple nights, when every noise would make me jump out of my skin and run for a kitchen knife. When I did sleep that night, I woke up startled to find Logan staring at me. I had forgotten that I was in the middle of a lovers' tryst. It was still dark in the room and his hair was disheveled.

"You have blue eyes," he said.

I nodded my head, staring into his face. He looked gorgeous.

"They're awesome," he said. He closed his eyes. "Do you know what it would feel like to have sex, Drew?"

I shook my head sleepily. "I don't even want you to *want* to have sex with me."

He wiggled his eyebrows. "Too late. I do. C'mon, you haven't thought about it?"

I wanted to tell Burt to take that surfboard and shove it, but a pink board was still better than no board at all.

"Well, yeah, but—"

"It would feel so good . . . "

I closed my eyes and pressed against him. "It's not going to happen," I said.

"No, it's not. That would be bad."

"Yeah, it would."

He kissed my forehead. "You're so different, Drew. You're so sweet and pretty and . . ."

"Quixotic?" I suggested sleepily.

Logan laughed. "Whatever the hell that means." He paused. "I've been thinking about what I'm going to take away from this experience, Drew."

"And?"

"Well, I think I'm going to walk away knowing that there are still good things out there. Not the entire world is made up of bullshit."

I smiled to myself and kissed his earlobe.

"Why do you like me?" he whispered.

I wrapped my arms around his middle and suddenly wondered what I was doing. "I honestly don't know," I said.

I dreamt that I was surfing with Logan, and each wave came bowing before me with foam hands extended, until I fell off my board like a baby rocking itself out

I watched Logan's lips as he talked, his voice filling me. I interrupted him by closing my mouth over his . . .

of its own cradle. And then Logan was pulling off my bathing suit, and when I got home my father was there asking why I had just been raped, and by the way, why did I smell like marijuana?

I woke up to my mother's face. She was yanking up my blinds with tear-stained cheeks, and the second I opened my eyes she was yelling.

"I trust you and this is what you do!" she screamed. Before I even realized Logan was still there, he was jumping out of bed and pulling on his jeans and stammering like a nine-year-old. My mother yelled after him even as he jumped into his van and peeled away.

"I can't believe this," she kept saying. I went to the bathroom, and then followed her to her room as she pulled out her weathered old suitcase and began throwing underwear and bras into it. "You're dead, Drew," she said. "You're so dead. How could you have some strange *man* in this house? Are you crazy? Are you completely crazy?"

I picked up a clump of panties from the floor and threw them at her. "You're one to talk!" I cried. I watched her face turn pale pink. "At least I didn't leave you alone for eight days! I didn't leave on your freaking birthday, Mom! No, I'm definitely not the one who did that."

When I turned to leave, she grabbed hold of my arm. "I asked you if it was OK with you, Drew, and you said it was. I'm not a mind reader, you know! I can't be perfect!"

"Yeah, well, that's obvious, Mom."

I watched her mouth form into a tiny, furious "O." Her fingers released my arm like it was suddenly covered with worms.

"It's true," I said, clearing my throat. "You're not even trying, Mom. You don't understand. I have *no one*. *No one* is looking out for me. I'm sixteen. I'm supposed to have parents, but I don't. I don't have anyone."

"That's ridiculous, Drew," she spat, turning her back to me as she emptied yet another drawer of clothes. "That is so unfair. You know I try, you know it. I'm sorry I can't be *everything*. I can't be your father's little flower child baking bread all day. I just can't. How am I sup-

I looked down at Logan's huge hands and said his age in my head. When I was six, he was losing his virginity; when I was ten, he was graduating from high school.

posed to be everything, huh? I can't do anything right, I guess. That's the way it is, I guess." She sniffed and ran the backside of her hand over her eyes. "Go pack up, Drew. We're leaving. I can't stand it here anymore. We're getting out of here."

I stood motionless, waiting for my mother's words to change in midair and come floating over to me, new and improved. When they didn't change, I collapsed in a lumpy heap on the floor. I cried like I did that day at Devereaux Point, when I was conquered by the tar.

I think she watched me for a little while. And then she sat down next to me and put her long, soft arm around my shoulders and stroked my hair back from my face.

"You know it's hard for me, Drew," she said softly, rocking me back and forth.

"It's hard for me too," I sobbed. "And all you do is sleep with different guys and get money and it's . . . it's terrible." I was hyperventilating and crying, and I wanted to evaporate and never return, unless it was to the ocean to ride wave after wave after wave . . .

"Shh . . . shh . . ." She brushed my hair behind my ears. "I *don't*, Drew. I really don't. You don't understand what it's like for me. It's not fun being alone, Drew. It's really not."

That's right, I wouldn't know a thing about being alone. I leaned into her chest and tried to slow down my breathing. My face was hot with tears.

"I hate Burt," I said.

I felt Mom nod. "I know, sweetie. I hate him too."

I looked up at her, questioning, and was surprised by how much anger I found in her face. She tightened her arms around me and leaned her head close to mine.

"Sweetie, sometimes you might think a certain guy is the one, the right one, and then he does something . . . I mean, you can't just fall for someone and expect him to be perfect, because . . . especially when sex is involved, because you're really too young for that, and I really am furious that you could possibly do something like this, when there're so many risks and dangers involved—"

I pulled away from her. "What are you talking about? I didn't have sex with him, Mom. I *can* think for myself, thank you very much."

Mom watched me as I stood and walked over to her bed, staring at the mound of G-string underwear thrown haphazardly into her suitcase. I thought of my father that day, holding his suitcase on the front stoop, shaking and stammering. And Mom, sitting next to my surfboard, talking about sacrifices.

"That was really stupid of me," I said in a low voice. "I shouldn't have let him in. I shouldn't have been hanging out with him."

"You could have been *raped*, Drew," Mom said, her eyes wide. "Or something even worse. I mean, am I that much of a failure? Have I been *that* terrible?"

I regarded her sadly, curled up in the doorway with her little red face and the huge blue eyes that I refused to see as mine. She had wrinkles around her mouth and creases in her forehead, and I wondered if this was the closest she would ever come to taking true responsibility for her actions.

I sat quiet as a meadow, my spirit folded neatly in my lap. It had tiny, frail butterfly wings that looked ready to fly away.

"I love you," I said softly. "But I think I need to live with Dad for a while. I think I need to be a normal kid. At least for a while. Don't you think it would help, Mom? If you could be on your own for a while?"

She responded by rising to her feet and walking away from me.

We didn't speak the whole way to Dad's. Mom put on her Joni Mitchell CD and perfected her stoical look while I stared out the window and bit my thumbnail until it bled. I thought about Logan, about things we did and his face that night telling me that I was sweet and pretty and different. But the more I thought about him, the more I just felt sick to my stomach and disappointed in myself that I couldn't have just walked away from it, from the whole situation. He was now my bittersweet secret, dissolving like sugar in water.

When we got to Dad's house, near UCSB where he worked, Mom turned to me and kissed my cheek. She

carried my stuff into the house, still not speaking, and I heard her suck in her breath when Susan opened the door. The "deflowered flower child" wasn't barefoot or wearing a poncho, like I expected. Her pale blonde hair was cut short and she had on loafers and jeans. When she hugged me I stiffened up like a defensive sea creature and thought of Mom's long, baby-soft arms.

My father got tears in his eyes. He laughed at my surfboard and said, "Pink, Drew? Is this a joke or have you changed drastically since I knew you last?"

Mom gave me a fierce hug goodbye and almost choked on her tears. She always said crying made her face puffy and that's why she never did it. But she drove away with wet cheeks, and when I went to my new bedroom my heart was pounding and I tried to calm myself by thinking of the lull of the tide and the gentle lapping of the water under my board.

The next day Dad took me to get my license, and I decided the first place I was going to drive to was More Mesa, the nude beach. I went at twilight, when it was practically deserted, and sat in the sand for almost an hour. Just as the sun was becoming a faint dying ember on the horizon, I stripped down to my underwear and ran into the water. I coiled my long hair into two Princess Leia buns and wrote "Drew, Warrior Princess" in the sand. And then I put on my T-shirt and grabbed my board for one last set before dark. I paddled out to the waves, cradled in the solitary sweetness of the sky. ★

Letter to My Father

i would like to write a poem for my father
but every time i start i get so frightened that i have
    to gather blankets and write a poem to me instead.

the first line of the poem-letter i start for you,
    father, is always:
my face is wet: snot tears and plastic make an ugly
    sound across pennsylvania and california
and then i am led to apologize again:
i am sorry about the noise, father, and about the wet.
i am sorry that i am crying at you.
how unfair.
i am sorry that i don't call.

here is the scrawny ink pen that made these stains
    on my fingers
here. see?
just under the knuckle on the middle finger.
and here the slight scratch in the desk from where
    i was too emphatic
and an exclamation point cut the wood.

the letter was returned, stamped
addressee unknown.
i read the letter myself,
    so that someone would have heard me.

enclosed please find:
    my first line of poetry
    my first-grade report card
    my first school picture.
i would be sending a clip from my first haircut
    but i have never needed one
    and this is why:
you can see from the photograph that i have oil-
    prone hair but it is soft when washed.
you can see from the photograph that i have
    narrow edges and empty eyes.

when i was very young i needed softness:
i yanked out my hair in clumps and held it,
    long and graceful, in my fist.
stuck my thumb in my mouth and rubbed my upper lip
with the smooth comforting ends of my hair.
it smelled of shampoo and toddler sweat.

i signed with sincerity and a good deal of release,
a leaking and sprawling signature,
your loving daughter.

—*Nava Etshalom,*
Twelfth grade, Masterman School,
Philadelphia, Pennsylvania

[*Other works by Nava Etshalom appear on pages 9 and 58.*]

desert trumpet

By Coco Krumme

contemporary
FICTION

Starbeams settle, and a pale day is shoved into life. The sun is born over the cracked earth of Death Valley, and the sky fades into a faint, swooning blue, almost white. White as birth, I remember thinking, and tainted with a bloody red sun. Our red Chevy pickup shoots out of California Highway 190's tunnel and drives into Death Valley.

My mother and I rarely left our San Francisco apartment to carve out the roads of southern California in our old Chevrolet, yet there we were, roaming the desert amid the ebbs and thrusts of late August. The trip was to be our epilogue, although we could never say so directly. My mother was dying of leukemia. Cancer lounged on her cheeks, choked her veins, and slowed her heart, and even now silence was her excuse and her shield. As we drove through the taciturn heat, I tried to ignore the chemotherapy's watermark on my mother's naked skull. She looked half-infant, half-skeleton. Convinced that her reticence protected me from pain, my mother had forgotten that cancer is airborne—the sorrow is contagious even without words.

In the desert you are alone. There might be lizards in the dead grass or cars that whisper past you, but your thoughts are inescapable and interminable. Breathe in the hot still air; look off a cliff and marvel at the insect cars scratching out the roads of this immensity. You can drag your feet in the parched sand and vow to fly, but Death Valley grabs ahold of its visitors, binding them to its dust and its splendor.

My mother was a great trumpet player in her day, when her lungs could still hold enough air. I guess I never really knew her, because she told her story in tones that only a musician could understand. In her time a woman jazz musician was an aberration, but her pulse beat triplets and dotted eighths, and she played in the anonymity and genderlessness of a big band. But even this song had its rallentando as it neared the end of its measure, and not even a musical genius could protect my mother from its ceasing.

At the fossilized old station where we stopped to get gas, we stretched our legs and opened dried peaches, pancakes from that morning's breakfast, bags of almonds, sodas, and huge canteens of water.

My mother turned to the desert-hardened man pumping gas. "You get a lot of business out here?" she asked.

"Some," he answered. "It's the desert, though, ma'am, and not a lot of folks live 'round here. Mostly tourists passing by."

"Yeah, it seems pretty isolated."

"Isolated, maybe. Never lonely, though." He lifted the dripping nozzle out of our tank.

"Where're you all from?" he asked. Who knows, who cares? It's always been this way, my mother and I alone in our San Francisco apartment or driving through the desert. My father, just a man passing through, the low note in an arpeggio rolling to its peak. The past, I've come to believe, is as irrelevant and malleable as the future. We pick and choose our memories, just as we like to believe we mold our future.

That afternoon we passed a gray coyote lying a few feet from the road. He was panting under his shaggy, worn coat.

"Let's stop," I begged my mother. "Look, he's thirsty."

"No, honey, it'll be fine. I'm sure he knows how to find water."

"How can you say that? He's going to die of thirst!"

"I told you, it'll be fine. It's not our business to meddle in nature's will." She gripped the steering wheel and focused intently on the black road ahead.

"Please, Mom. We have plenty of water. We can't just let him die here in the desert."

"Animals know how to survive in the wilderness; it's instinctual for them." She glanced over at me. "Look, if it means so much to you, we can go back. But what will giving it water do—just postpone its death?"

The gods of life and death tell me she's dying, seeping back into the hard earth of the valley.

I was silent, and the Chevy didn't hesitate or lose speed. We kept driving with 'survival of the fittest' thick in our throats, but the thirsty coyote lingered in my memory.

When the chemotherapy began, my mother started praying, secretly. A leather-bound Bible, probably stolen from a hotel room or picked up at a yard sale, lay morosely on her bedside table. I heard psalms pulsating on her lips, and prayers to Jesus and Mother Mary; she harbored rosary beads in her hands and in her heart. I thought I saw a gold cross against her breast, but maybe it was just a mirage, or another Medic Alert chain. In the desert too we are haunted by mirages. Not indigo oases, but ghosts of possible futures, words we should say to each other but leave behind in fear.

I never wanted this to be a Southwestern story, with cacti standing guard and tumbleweed blowing through these black-and-white rows. No, this is my story. This is my love and this is my life; I offer no flaming peppers and gunshots at high noon. These too are desert mirages; they boil away when the sun rises, leaving only the bitter minerals of life.

We circled the entire valley that day, inhaling its dusty secrets and admiring its grave beauty. It grew late, and we decided to look for a campground for the night. Eventually, we found a square of land with scattered tent stakes and an assortment of water fountains jutting out of the earth, a place called Seven Palms. There wasn't a speck of green, much less a palm tree, in sight—only the dry hard earth. My mother rolled the red Chevy into one of the angular plots, then went to the manager's trailer to check in and pay the three dollars.

As I waited for her, I looked out across the valley and wondered how much longer my mother would live. She seemed healthy enough, and there was her shadow moving firmly on the earth, the solid, steady earth. Yet here I was, horseless and gunless in the Wild West, with my mother half-dead, as they say. The infamous 'they,' gods of life and death. They tell me she's dying, seeping back into the hard earth of the valley. They pump salt into her body, the body that gave me life, and watch dumbly as that salt tumbles out in her tears. Just watch, her hair will fall out! they decree. We'll put chemicals into her veins and postpone death, like gods. Of course, they confess, everyone has to die someday. For who is immune to the fate that not even science can control? But here in Death Valley, she cannot admit to me that she's dying.

My mother returned, and we decided to go for a hike before putting up our tent. As we walked eastward, I could feel the setting sun on my back. The slanting light threw a supine beam across the valley, and the hillside's shadow behind us inched toward our footprints. In front of us the evening had painted twin shadows on the sand—a mother's and a daughter's. The sun sank, and the two black reflections reached farther and farther, and, for an instant, hit infinity. Then, in harmony with the sunset, the shadows disappeared.

As we walked back to Seven Palms in the blue twilight, I wondered if the sapphire of evening was a postponement of darkness or simply nature's routine. On a whim, or perhaps intoxicated by the beauty of the twilight and the brevity of life, my mother grasped my hand and squeezed it with deep love. Words we could not say will always haunt us, and the black of night fell without fail, but in darkness we lit a candle to soften the sorrow. And somewhere in that valley of dust and death, the flame still shines. ★

THERE BUT
FOR THE GRACE

BY
MIA CABANA

I play the clarinet. I feel like shouting that from a rooftop sometimes. My band director has a little framed card on his desk that says, I MAKE MY LIVING TEACHING MUSIC. The first time I read it I thought it was dumb. I mean, it didn't even rhyme or anything. Then after a little while I realized that it was a simple, proud declaration. Like saying, I MAKE MY LIVING TEACHING MUSIC—IS THERE ANY BETTER WAY TO SPEND A LIFE?

I'm on my second clarinet now. It's made of wood, so it gets a better sound. Its name is Walter. My first clarinet was Joe. He was plastic and faithful and abused. I started playing in fifth grade. I've been playing for almost six years now. In sixth grade the middle school band director sat me next to Mark Binsley. He's been my stand partner ever since. By now he's my best friend, too. He's one of three people in the world who have heard me play in the last three years.

In seventh grade I played a concert in a church—it was Beethoven's *Minuet in G*—and my clarinet (Joe) wouldn't stop squeaking. All through the piece, *dee-dee-dee-de-SQUAK*. I got really upset and started to cry, right there on the stage in front of God and everyone. Pretty soon I got the hiccups, and then it was *dee-dee-hic-dee-SQUAK*. By the time I was done, I was in subdued hysterics. I stood up, barely able to see anything because of the blurry tears. My nose was leaking down my face. With one last horrible hiccup of defeat, I ran from the stage, sobbing. Ever since then I've refused to play for anyone. Even my parents. If they're home when I play, I practice in a closet.

Clarinets are very scary. Sometimes I wish I could yell that from a rooftop, too. Somewhere in between my hiccups and closet I got good, though. Even better than Mark Binsley (I always call him by both his names, just because they fit together so nicely). Mark Binsley used to sit on my right side, signifying his higher standing on

the great band food chain. Musical superiority. Last two years, he's sat on my left.

I came into band on Monday and read the Joke of the Day on the board: *Why do bagpipers walk when they play? To get away from the noise.* I laughed. It's a musician's joke. Sometimes Mark and I try telling them to our other friends who aren't in the band. They never get them. There was a new piece on our stand, "Amazing Grace." Mark Binsley was already playing it. Flawlessly. Mark sight-reads so well it makes me want to kick him. Sometimes I do.

"It's a nice arrangement," he pronounces his verdict. I decide not to kick him. We always decide whether a new piece is a "good song" or not. If it's a "good" one, no matter how hard it is we'll practice until it's perfect and relish every minute of it. Mr. Hun taps his baton on the stand for attention.

"John Newton," he announces, "wrote this song in 1779. He worked on a slave ship and wrote this song after having an epiphany about slavery. This could be on the quiz." Mark gets scared when he hears the word "quiz" and jots notes on the top of our music in his quirky, Mark Binsley way. I laugh at what he's written. It says "John Newton. Slave guy. Wrote stuff."

We play the piece through once. There are a whole bunch of tiny solos in weird, exposed places. I have one of them. Mark Binsley cues me when to play, just because he's my stand partner and stand partners do stuff like that for each other. I come in at the wrong time a lot anyway. Mr. Hun tells us at the end of rehearsal that we will be playing "Amazing Grace" in the MICA Festival competition in two weeks. Sometimes my mom says, "There but for the grace of God go I." It means that any minute you could be in the other person's shoes. Fate's way of saying, "Subject to change without notice." "I once was lost but now I'm found; was blind but now I see."

There's one part in the piece where the clarinets have the melody, beautiful and clear. The high C note feels so tentative, like it might just switch from being a high C to a squeak at any second. It feels like if you can just hang on to that note, sustain it, the world will be perfect for a few seconds. We sound like bagpipes at that part, I tell Mark. I have a tape recording of bagpipe music from my mother's friend who lives

MEMOIR

in Scotland and came to visit us the summer when I was nine. "Amazing Grace" is the first song on the second side. Bagpipe music gives me chills. I draw a picture on the top of the page of a guy playing bagpipes. Mark Binsley labels it "John Newton."

For two weeks we practice "Amazing Grace" and some other pieces. Then the day of the festival arrives. We all load onto the bus and go to Trenton High, one hour away. Trenton is one of those offbeat artistic

The high C note feels so tentative . . . It feels like if you can just hang on to that note, sustain it, the world will be perfect for a few seconds.

schools. I'd never been in the high school before. There are murals all over the walls. A lady with a nose ring and big jangly bracelets brings us to a room where we're supposed to set up. Mark Binsley and most of the rest of the band leave to get lunch or listen to the other groups play. Everyone is gone except for me and Pete Webster. Pete plays the drums and is infinitely adorable. We're almost-friends. Pete is short, and I think he must have gotten picked on a lot when he was little. To make up for it, he wields blinding sarcasm as a weapon, loaded with cynicism for ammo. But he's never directly mean to me. I guess it's just his way of dealing with being scared. Like me, hiding in a closet when I play.

We sit around in the warmup room for a while. I share my orange with him and show him the Gary Larson cartoon I taped in our music folder this morning. I wrote "Mark Binsley and Rita" on the top. It's a picture of two prisoners hanging in manacles from a dungeon wall. The caption reads, "No, you idiot! Now this time wait for me to finish the first 'row row row your boat' *before* you come in!" Pete laughs. We walk around the halls for a while, looking at all the murals. Then we go back to the warmup room. It's noisy, and everyone is running around trying to get ready. I help Pete button his top shirt button and fix his tie. My fingers shake so hard I almost can't do it, and I can't explain why.

I go get in line with Mark Binsley and we tune up. Mark is always out of tune. It's not his fault—it's his clarinet. He's supposed to be getting a new mouthpiece to fix it. Then we are on stage. I'm staring at the pattern of bricks that makes up the backstage wall, as if memorizing it might make everything perfectly clear and

rational. Mark finds the cartoon and laughs.

There are a bunch of people in the auditorium. We play a march to warm up, and then a fast piece. The audience claps for us. Then it's time for "Amazing Grace." It starts out slow and low, then there is just a hint of the melody (this is the part that the audience recognizes, and they let out a barely audible "ooh" of acknowledgement). Then comes my lonely open part. Out of the corner of my eye I see Mark Binsley getting ready to point, but I don't need him to. I know right where I am. Suddenly things don't seem so scary, and before you know it I'm hearing Mark come in next to me and it's over.

I want to put down my clarinet and shout from the stage right there, "Hey! Hey, everyone! I just came out of the closet!" But I don't because it would screw up our performance and who knows what kind of things Pete would say about me, not to mention how all of the Trentonites in the audience might take it the wrong way. And maybe that's not the type of thing you *should* shout. Maybe that's the type of thing that needs to echo around inside you. Like bagpipe music.

We get to the high C and I hold it as if my life depends on it. Sometimes Mark Binsley and I have telepathic moments when we play the same thing the same way without even discussing it. I try sending my thoughts: "Hey, Mark, why do clarinetists sit in closets when they play? To get away from the noise." I laugh inside myself at this, and the laughter kind of ricochets off my insides and gets mixed up with my shouting for joy and the high C and everything.

Then it's all very quiet and we're fading out, soft and low. The rule is that if you run out of breath, you just stop playing. Mark Binsley always lasts longer than I do. I sit still after my instrument stops making sound, and listen to the last vibrations die around me. John Newton. Slave guy. Wrote stuff. Knew more about freedom than he thought he did.

Rita—ME! Closets. Play clarinet. Know a lot more about freedom now, too. I look up and smile at Pete across the stage; he smiles back. I look at the lady with the nose ring who is standing in the wings. Mr. Hun's hands are still up, even though there really isn't any more music happening—at least any you can hear. Mark Binsley kicks me playfully in the foot. I agree. It's a good song. ★

About Our Cover . . .

What's up with the wordy whale on Merlyn's cover? Look closely and you may recognize some of these seemingly random sentences as opening lines from great novels. In fact, the entire whale, head to tail, is covered with opening lines. How many can you find and identify? Visit Merlyn online at www.merlynspen.com to learn more about Ken Vaudrain, the artist, and to enter our Whale Watch Contest.

Discussion

The Pongee Stick

By Alex Taylor (p. 6)

1. Bitter, Kevin views himself as a victim of circumstance. How is it that people like Kevin and his buddies "give up," while others less fortunate, like Holocaust survivor Elie Wiesel and paralyzed actor Christopher Reeve, do not?

2. Sensuous images (" . . . his lips squirmed into the receiver") and hard-hitting similes (" . . . fed to the gooks like fodder in slow, methodical feasts") help bring the country and its unwelcome guests into sharp focus. Find and discuss other descriptive details that enable you to visualize the action and settings. Notice the contrast of lush, innocent jungle with the warring intrusions of man.

Virginia Mud

By Loraine Reitman (p. 14)

1. Have you any idea what's happening in the pond and in the swimmer's mind? Compare your own interpretation(s) with those of your classmates. Was Chase present? Why did she stay underwater so long? Why give condolences to Shirley?

2. Did the author succeed in sucking you into the Virginia mud, along with the narrator? That is, did the heavy yet spacey mood leech out and somehow touch you? What were your thoughts and feelings as you read? Could you empathize with any aspect of this essentially unknowable woman? How so, or not so?

Lucky

By Joseph Reynolds (p. 18)

1. Explosive, true-to-life dialogue is just one of the ways this author builds suspense around the footlocker incident. What else does he do to bring you into the awful here-and-now of Lucky's no-win predicament? What do you see and sense that contributes to the tension and causes you to care?

2. Private Luck eventually discovers that his bigoted and seemingly irrational "superiors" have set him up—in a kind of pugilistic interview—to establish pecking order. Have you, too, ever faced a challenge that was initially veiled, secret, or simply of unclear origin? Ever been "tested" as the brunt of a practical joke?

The Felicity Maker

By Dan Kahn (p. 24)

1. Under the Weatherdome, people are far less aware than even Truman of *The Truman Show*. Are there areas in *your* life also—beliefs, attitudes, fears, etc.—that you may have more or less "inherited," and that you embrace as uncritically as do the Hendersons and their neighbors? Select one for study and written analysis.

2. Can you envision any kind of felicity that does not depend upon the coexistence of its opposite, infelicitous force? That is, can there be beauty without the contrast of ugliness, compassion without pain, joy without sorrow? What is *your* definition of felicity? Do you agree with the Felicity Maker that it cannot be pure?

The Gift of Life

By Sam Hancock (p. 35)

1. The author affects a kind of mock formality in his word choices. Would you say that this style sharpens—or detracts from—the humor and flow? That is, what effect does the super-dignified presentation have upon the burlesque events it describes?

2. Family members and friends are shown in all their blemished glory—hair-trigger Dad, oblivious fiancé, rascally sister, clueless playmates. Even so, some readers find that these characters come off as strangely lovable. What, to you, makes them likable, unlikable, or somewhere in between? Has the author's "tone" something to do with it?

Crossing the Street

By Johanna Povirk-Zhoy (p. 38)

1. Timid, deferential, and repressed, Mother has somehow lost meaningful contact with her daughter. Considering Mother's homelife, words, and actions, as well as Margie's temperament, can you intuit what may've led to the split—and how it was so quickly mended?

2. McCarthyism. Unliberated housewives and their ladylike daughters. Lazy summer days with nothing to do. The dawn of rock 'n' roll. Segregated restrooms. Do the Fifties look like "*good old days*"? How so, or not so? Are *our* times any more or less in line with your idea of the good life than Margie's?

December 1773

By Rebecca Scott (p. 46)

1. Outwardly neutral, Edith swings from loyalist to rebel as a revolutionary idea takes root in her mind/heart. Search your own life's experiences for a time(s) when you, too, and/or people you know, dared to challenge the status quo. What happened? Try to fairly and evenly present two or more sides of the situation.

2. History outweighs fiction in this piece of historical fiction as more attention is given to *Zeitgeist* 1773 (the spirit of the times) than to plot and suspense (mother's illness; the possibility of being orphaned) or characterization (showing what makes the characters tick). Is this, to you, a weakness? An artistic necessity? Defend your preference for this story "as is" or for further development.

Chance of a Lifetime

By Evan Grosshans (p. 51)

1. After a silent reading, have three volunteers take on the roles of Ordinary Boy and Ordinary Girl. Does the acted-out play leave you with different thoughts and impressions of the play? If so, what do you think made the difference?

2. What do you see as the central philosophical and/or psychological issue(s) in "Chance of a Lifetime"? Is there one? Several? Have you encountered them yourself in real life? Do the characters reach consensus on any of them?

Fire and Water

By Jim Cady (p. 53)

1. Does the narrator's innocent, eleven-year-old "voice" sound authentic to you? If so, find passages that ring especially true to the feelings and outlook of a little boy in his situation. Are there any off-notes, moments that do not ring true?

2. The role of television in defining this child's physical, emotional, and even spiritual reality is a theme that helps weave the story together. Like an always-on TV set, droning in the background, its presence is felt continuously. What are some of the more salient "lessons" imparted to this lonely little boy by his electronic parent?

Separation

By Sarah Fahey (p. 61)

1. Midway through the story, as he is boxing his mother's religious effects, Liam contrasts his own mother with the Blessed Mother. Try to restate, in simpler and more obvious words, the meaning of his scathing characterization of Mom and his irreverent description of Mother Mary.

2. Imagine: Martians and Venusians are observing Liam through the tool shed window. Nonplussed, they watch as he kicks the sawdust, fumbles with useless old tools, and jams bent nails and scraps of paper into his pocket. "What on Earth?" they demand to know. How do you explain Liam's actions?

The Glue Jar

By Aarti Gupta (p. 64)

1. Reluctant to offer her canned condolence, the little girl thinks, *This doesn't feel right.* What do you think feels wrong? Experiment: Try to go for a full hour without telling any white lies! For example, if it's not so, don't say "fine" in response to "How are you?" Get real! Report your findings and feelings to the class.

2. With clarity and candor, the author speaks in the refreshing and *authentic* voice of her six-year-old self—an innocently self-centered self. Still, with the passage of time comes "residual guilt." What might that guilt consist of? Is the guilt authentic? Justified? A mannerly add-on? Something else?

The East Pole

By Jenny Smith (p. 67)

1. "Normal life" has shut down—not only in the snowy streets, but also for the Pierce family and for the minister who must break the news of Mr. Pierce's death to his children. How does this quiet interval, this stoppage, seem to alter the narrator's view of the world, both inside herself and outside?

2. The East Pole. Shangri-la. East of Eden. Hicksville, USA. Choose one of these allegorical places (or create your own) as the setting for a vignette, poem, song or story that conveys something about the human condition as you see it—or wish it were.

Sweaty Palms

By Daniel Becker (p. 69)

1. Very few of us can escape feelings of nervousness and anxiety when it comes to revealing our feelings for a potential boyfriend or girlfriend. Who has not been tormented by the question, "Should I call him (her)? What if he (she) rejects me?" What do you think is behind this very common fear? Do some people seem to suffer it more than others?

2. In real life, as in this story, tragedy and comedy commingle. Still, some readers regard the double death in Jonah's family as a too-heavy cloud that shadows—or makes improbable—the jolly times that follow. Do you share this view? How do you explain Jonah's lively, un-self-pitying behavior?

Drew, Warrior Princess

By Keleigh Friedrich (p. 75)

1. Like any good warrior, Drew keeps a tight lid on her hurt and angry feelings. Find passages that show, in both physical and mental ways, how (and sometimes why) she maintains her "stiff upper lip." Does "Warrior Princess" seem any more or less true of her *after* the "battle" with Mom? How so, or not so?

2. The sad spectacle of Mom—immature, deluded, well-intentioned—makes for a fascinating character study, especially as seen through the harsh lens of her daughter. Clearly, though, Mom's view of herself is much more forgiving. See if you can BE Mom, if only for the time it takes you to write a letter to Drew. Describe "your" (Mom's) feelings and new realizations, if any.

Desert Trumpet

By Coco Krumme (p. 86)

1. The narrator's view of Death Valley is rife with "pathetic fallacy." (Look up the term if you're unfamiliar with it.) Find a few instances of these humanlike appearances and actions, and ask yourself: Do they complement and/or amplify the feelings of the narrator? Do they help set a mood? How so, or not so?

2. Does the musical motif, with its many terms and metaphors, serve an artistic purpose? Could any other theme relating to Mom's vocation/avocation (say, "Desert Quiche" if she were a chef; "Desert Plié" for a ballet-dancing mom) have been equally affecting? Rewrite one of the "musical paragraphs" (satirically or seriously) using the theme of your choice. Does it "work"?

There But for the Grace

By Mia Cabana (p. 88)

1. How would you describe the relationship between Rita and Mark Binsley? Romance is not in the air. They don't necessarily seem to be the kinds of friends who get together after school. Yet, it's suggested that they are a near-perfect duo! How so? Does this kind of kinship have a name or special significance? Would you be drawn to Rita and/or Mark as a friend? How so, or not so?

2. What factors led to the protagonist's ultimate emergence from the clarinet closet? Do you think her own strength of will was the greater force? Could it also have had something to do with the music itself? If you have ever overcome a particular fear, what did you do, dare, or dream that brought you victory?

—Discussion Starters by Jo-Ann Langseth

Essay Contests

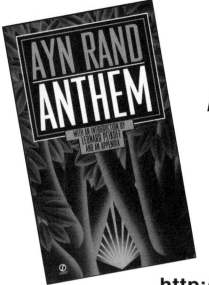

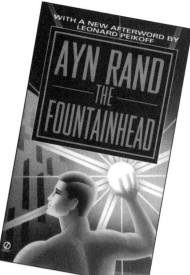

$35,000
in Prize Money

47 Prizes

Top Prize $10,000

http://www.aynrand.org/contests/

For 9th and 10th Graders:
8th Annual Essay Contest on Ayn Rand's Novelette

ANTHEM
Entry Deadline: April 1, 2000

1998–99 Prize Winners:

$1,000 First Prize:
Joseph W. Saba, Hanover Area Jr./Sr. H.S., Wilkes Barre, PA

$200 Second Prizes:
Robert W. Cobbs, St. Anselm's Abbey School, Washington, DC
Dylan Davey, Stone Ridge School of the Sacred Heart, Bethesda, MD
Jessica Solomon, Grosse Pointe North H.S., Grosse Pointe Woods, MI
Nirav Vora, Myers Park H.S., Charlotte, NC
Rebecca Knapp, The Academy for the Advancement of Science & Technology, Hackensack, NJ
Hila Katz, Ward Melville H.S., East Setauket, NY
Jessica Singleton, Friends Seminary H.S., New York, NY
Tiffany Pasquariello, Seaford H.S., Seaford, NY
Shilpi Agarwal, Clear Lake H.S., Houston, TX
Katherine Bach-Mai Vu, Clear Lake H.S., Houston, TX

$100 Third Prizes:
Sarah Hicks, Buena H.S., Sierra Vista, AZ
Vanessa Stephan, Grand Junction H.S., Grand Junction, CO
Nadia Al-Khatib, Choate Rosemary Hall, Wallingford, CT
Lance Garrett, Miami Sunset Senior, Miami, FL
Sandra Jackson, Spruce Creek H.S., Port Orange, FL
Katie Davis, Newton H.S., Covington, GA
Jordan Krause, Centre H.S., Lost Springs, KS
Vikas Goela, Phillips Academy, Andover, MA
Philip Moser, Fellowship Christian Academy, Methuen, MA
Crystal Gammon, School of the Osage H.S., Kaiser, MO
Bryce Kahle, Lincoln East H.S., Lincoln, NE
Miling Yan, Lincoln East H.S., Lincoln, NE
Kevin J. Deanna, Cedar Grove H.S., Cedar Grove, NJ
Jason Jennings, Cherry Hill H.S. West, Cherry Hill, NJ
Elizabeth Melly, Lower Dauphin H.S., Hummelstown, PA
Heather Lucas, Fox Chapel Area H.S., Pittsburgh, PA
Helen McLendon, White Station H.S., Memphis, TN
Chad Cumba, Clear Lake H.S., Houston, TX
Kristen McAlear, Clear Lake H.S., Houston, TX
Erica Fuss, Holmen H.S., Holmen, WI

For 11th and 12th Graders:
15th Annual Essay Contest on Ayn Rand's Novel

THE FOUNTAINHEAD
Entry Deadline: April 15, 2000

1998–99 Prize Winners:

$10,000 First Prize:
Boleslaw Z. Kabala, Groton School, Groton, MA

$2,000 Second Prizes:
Alex Zuckerman, North Hollywood H.S., N. Hollywood, CA
Matthew McDermott, The Louisiana School for Math, Science and the Arts, Natchitoches, LA
John Perich, Loyola Blakefield H.S., Towson, MD
Rachana Vajjhala, Fox Chapel Area H.S., Pittsburgh, PA
Melissa Bailey, James E. Taylor H.S., Katy, TX

$1,000 Third Prizes:
Christon Smith, A. P. Brewer H.S., Somerville, AL
Stephanie Erin Brewer, Masuk H.S., Monroe, CT
Lauren Davis, Stanton College Prep. School, Jacksonville, FL
Ann Yribar, Bishop Kelly H.S., Boise, ID
Yuan Wang, Phillips Academy, Andover, MA
John Eric Howell - II, Lamar Foundation H.S., Meridian, MS
Laura K. Nuffer, Horace Greeley H.S., Chappaqua, NY
Adrianne J. Pasquarelli, Rhinebeck H.S., Rhinebeck, NY
Brian C. Henriksen, Harrisonburg H.S., Harrisonburg, VA
Ashwini Natraj, St. Xaviers College, Mumbai, India

Contest Information and Teacher Guides

To receive a free teacher's kit containing the contest information and the *Teacher's Guide to Anthem and The Fountainhead*, send your name and school address to:

**The Ayn Rand® Institute
P.O. Box 6004, Dept. MP
Inglewood, CA 90312**

Please allow 4–6 weeks for delivery, or receive your kit within two weeks by requesting materials on Web at:

http://www.aynrand.org/contests/kit/

Merlyn's Pen Order Form

Merlyn's products may also be ordered, conveniently and securely, at www.merlynspen.com.

BILL TO:

Name _____

Address _____

_____

City _____ State ____ Zip _____

Telephone: day (___) _____

Payment Method:

❏ Check or Money Order enclosed

❏ Bill School/District (Purchase Order must be enclosed.)

Purchase Order #_____

Make check payable to: Merlyn's Pen, Inc.

Mail to: Merlyn's Pen, Inc.
Dept. A00
P.O. Box 910
East Greenwich, Rhode Island 02818

SHIP TO: (if different)

Current Subscriber I.D. # (if known):_____

Attn:_____

Name _____

Address_____

_____

City_____ State_____ Zip _____

Please give a street address for shipping.

❏ MasterCard

❏ Visa

Card # _____

Expiration date_____

_____
Authorized Signature

Orders: (800) 247-2027
Fax: (401) 885-5222
E-mail: merlynspen@aol.com
website: www.merlynspen.com

Code	Title/Description	Quantity	Unit Price	Extended Price
	Merlyn's Pen Annual Edition, Vol. ____ (Specify code and volume.)			
	DISCARD			

*Rhode Island residents add 7% sales tax.

SHIPPING: 12% of subtotal.
        Minimum shipping charge $3.00.

Canada & Mexico: Shipping is 20% of subtotal. Minimum charge is $4.00. **Foreign:** Shipping is 30% of subtotal. Minimum shipping charge is $5.00. Orders must be **paid in U.S. funds.**

SUBTOTAL	$
Sales Tax (RI only)*	$
Shipping Charges**	$
ORDER TOTAL	$